CrackBerry

True Tales of BlackBerry Use and Abuse

Kevin Michaluk,
Martin Trautschold
and
Gary Mazo

Apress®

CrackBerry: True Tales of BlackBerry Use and Abuse

ISBN-13 (pbk): 978-1-4302-3180-6

ISBN-13 (electronic): 978-1-4302-3181-3

Printed and bound in the United States of America 9 8 7 6 5 4 3 2 1

President and Publisher: Paul Manning
Lead Editor: Steve Anglin
Development Editor: James Markham
Editorial Board: Clay Andres, Steve Anglin, Mark Beckner, Ewan Buckingham, Gary Cornell, Jonathan Gennick, Jonathan Hassell, Michelle Lowman, Matthew Moodie, Duncan Parkes, Jeffrey Pepper, Frank Pohlmann, Douglas Pundick, Ben Renow-Clarke, Dominic Shakeshaft, Matt Wade, Tom Welsh
Coordinating Editor: Laurin Becker
Copy Editor: Patrick Meador
Compositor: MacPS, LLC
Indexer: BIM Indexing & Proofreading Services
Cover Designer: Anna Ishchenko

Distributed to the book trade worldwide by Springer Science+Business Media, LLC., 233 Spring Street, 6th Floor, New York, NY 10013. Phone 1-800-SPRINGER, fax (201) 348-4505, e-mail orders-ny@springer-sbm.com, or visit www.springeronline.com.

For information on translations, please e-mail rights@apress.com, or visit www.apress.com.

Apress and friends of ED books may be purchased in bulk for academic, corporate, or promotional use. eBook versions and licenses are also available for most titles. For more information, reference our Special Bulk Sales–eBook Licensing web page at www.apress.com/info/bulksales.

For Erika, the #1 recovering BlackBerry addict in my life.
–Kevin Michaluk

For our families—our wives, Julie and Gloria, and to our kids, Sophie, Livvie and Cece, and Ari, Dan, Sara, Billy, Elise and Jonah.
–Martin Trautschold and Gary Mazo

For all BlackBerry users and abusers, without whom a work like this would go unappreciated!

Contents at a Glance

Contents

Acknowledgments

A book like this takes many people to put together. We would like to thank Apress for believing in us and our unique style of writing.

We would like to thank our Editors, Jim and Laurin, and the entire editorial team at Apress.

We would like to thank our families for their patience and support in allowing us to pursue projects such as this one.

Lastly, we thank both the CrackBerry.com community members and the Made Simple Learning customers who contributed stories to this book.

The Authors' Stories

Before we begin in earnest with our 12-step program, we're going to take a few pages to tell you our own stories of BlackBerry use and abuse. We suspect you will probably recognize yourself in many of our stories; in so doing, you may find that this book is the intervention you never knew you needed.

 **Gary's Story**

I have been using my BlackBerry for the least amount of time (compared to Martin and Kevin). I entered the BlackBerry world about four years ago. My training was actually as a member of the clergy—I am an ordained Rabbi—but my love of technology always seemed to permeate everything I did. I was known for using my personal digital assistant PDA (i.e., handheld computer) at funerals and weddings to help me remember my talking points. (Many services were outside, so the computer helped me avoid using paper that might fly away in the wind.) This worked great until they started adding phones to these PDAs. It wasn't so great when I forgot to turn off my phone ringer, and the "Star Wars Theme" rang out at graveside one day—much to the shocked stares of the grieving.

These days, I teach college courses on line for the University of Phoenix and work with Martin at Made Simple Learning as Partner, Vice President and co-author of our books. My busy life truly needs organization. One day a few years ago, a brand new BlackBerry Curve 8300 appeared for review on one of the websites I was writing for—and it was love at first roll of the trackball!

I came to rely on my BlackBerry Curve for just about everything. I set different tones to remind me to complete various tasks. These tones tell me what appointment is upcoming, who is calling, and even when text messages arrive from my family. My beloved BlackBerry is always ringing (usually with a movie theme or a rock song), and it often rings when and where it shouldn't. I try hard to remember to turn it off when riding my bike, on the golf course, at worship, or in the movies. But sometimes I forget, and it can be truly embarrassing.

The BlackBerry brought *push email* (see the Appendix A: "CrackBerry Terms and Definitions") to my world. And like all new BlackBerry users, I immediately became hooked on the instant gratification of getting my email wherever I was. Without realizing it, I developed a habit of looking for that little red light that indicates a new message has arrived about at least once a minute or so. I also found myself grabbing my BlackBerry each time the red light went off or the device vibrated—even when I was behind the wheel!

One day, I was driving with my oldest son, who had just received his driving permit. Without realizing it, I was driving the car, shifting the stick shift, adjusting the volume of the Bluetooth hands free, changing the channel on the remote of the satellite radio, and checking my email on the BlackBerry—all while traveling 40 MPH down a winding country road.

And I chose this moment to turn to my son and say, "Remember: When you drive, always keep your eyes on the road and be ready to react in an emergency." My son just laughed at me and shook his head. Obviously, I was doing so many things that my eyes and mind could not possibly be focused on the road. Thankfully, I have not had any accidents (yet), and I hope to avoid doing any more *texting while driving.* (See the true-life story about someone wrecking a Mercedes while using a BlackBerry in Chapter 1: "I Can't Be Without It").

In the last couple of years, Martin and I have branched out to write books about the iPad, iPhone, Palm Pre and soon the Droid. While all these devices have an element of addiction potential, I still find myself coming back "home" to whatever BlackBerry is on my desk or in my pocket – there is just something about these things! I hope you can learn a few things from this book that will help you curb your own BlackBerry uses and abuses.

 # Kevin's Story

My BlackBerry story began in 2005, when the release of the company's first real "consumer device" made BlackBerry became a household name. Prior to that, it was mainly just people in the corporate world who were aware of the device and having to grapple with BlackBerry addiction. My own introduction to the BlackBerry happened as it surely has for many others—it was given to me on the first day of a new job.

I went to work as a Business Development analyst for one of Canada's biggest media companies. Shortly after noon during my first day on the job, a tech guy from the IT department came down to my office and set me up with *old Blue*, the brick-like BlackBerry 7290. My training lesson was short. Here's the email, here's the phone, here's how you mark prior messages, and here's your phone number.

Although I also considered myself a gadget nut, I had no experience with BlackBerry smartphones prior to this first meeting. I first learned about the BlackBerry from a university case study that, ironically enough, was actually about a competitor: the Handspring Visor. A short time later, I became good friends with a guy who claimed to be addicted to his BlackBerry. (I had never really got to see my friend's BlackBerry close up—I should have realized then that its grasp was strong!) This was my first real, face-to-face encounter with what would ultimately become the focus of the next few years of my life.

At first meeting, I wasn't all that excited about the device. It was big compared to my streamlined Samsung flip phone. It also seemed kind of clunky, with an '80s look to it, despite the fact the year was 2005.

I wasn't all that excited by my new toy, and I was not yet that busy with my new job, so I left the big blue 'Berry on my desk for two days. On the third day after arriving at this new job, I noticed it again. Thinking the phone would be long dead, I went to charge it, but noticed then that the battery meter had barely moved. I remember thinking: "Wow, what a long battery life! Maybe there *is* something to this BlackBerry thing."

Once I finally picked up and used the device, the BlackBerry smartphone's hold on me was immediate and unshakable. I quickly mastered the ins-and-outs of the device. I couldn't believe how intuitive it was, nor how fast it was to use.

I took the BlackBerry everywhere with me—it was my newspaper in the stall during my morning bathroom breaks, my alarm clock in the bedroom, my entertainment during my commute (BrickBreaker skills extraordinaire), my way to kill time when waiting in line, and my distraction of choice when bored. The BlackBerry became my 24/7 companion who was always there for me, without exception. It was also my constant connection to my employer and work tasks, but I saw that as a good thing—it allowed me to get my job done better.

Although I didn't classify my reliance on the device as an addiction at that point, I knew I had become dependent on the BlackBerry when it was taken away after I left the company. I lasted all of four days before I had to buy my own personal BlackBerry to get my life get back to normal again.

> ### My girlfriend
> # Hated It!
> ### The BlackBerry was my
> ## Priority - Always

The BlackBerry was like electricity to me. I would never want to go back to life without it. But my blinders were on. I saw my BlackBerry as the greatest thing ever, but its features came at a significant cost. The BlackBerry became my priority—always. My girlfriend hated it. It didn't matter if we were watching a movie, out for dinner, or in the bedroom: we were never alone. The device was always at my side. If it vibrated, chirped, or blinked its red light, I was instantly reaching for it.

My coworkers hated the device. One time, I was out for lunch with everyone, telling a story with five minutes of setup. Then, in mid-sentence, I saw the red flashing light and stopped dead to grab my BlackBerry. I just left everybody hanging! And so it continued. My priority was the BlackBerry, and that meant that everything and everybody else was secondary.

> # *They just don't get it because they don't own a BlackBerry...*

Like many addicts, I didn't realize I had a problem. I didn't seek to control my addiction—I believed that *others* had the problem because they just "didn't get it." And they didn't get it because they *didn't have their own BlackBerry*. Being the helpful and caring guy that I am, I took care of the issue by buying my girlfriend a BlackBerry and convincing many of my non-BlackBerry using friends and colleagues to give the BlackBerry a try, as well.

As hard as the addiction hit me, it also took hold of everyone I introduced to the BlackBerry. I thought all my problems were solved: nobody seemed to mind me using my BlackBerry anymore because everyone else had their own BlackBerry smartphones, too. Communication with my friends also improved. We used BBM to tie us all together.

> # Maybe this Addiction thing was
> # REAL problem!

It was a few months after I bought my girlfriend a BlackBerry that it began to dawn on me that BlackBerry addiction was becoming a *real* problem. It wasn't an observation of my own behavior that spawned this revelation—no, I was a pro at justifying my own actions. Rather, it was an evening at home with my girlfriend, when I discovered she was more in the mood to play with her BlackBerry than in the mood to play with me. It was her BlackBerry addiction that was driving me nuts!

At this point, I knew I had to learn to control my BlackBerry use better, despite my love for the gadget. In so doing, I could show others the way (my girlfriend included), so this terrible incident would never happen again.

Martin's Story

My first exposure to the BlackBerry actually began in the fall of 2001. I was walking through a tradeshow floor in Atlanta with my brother-in-law, Ned Johnson. We were attending the show to help develop ideas to get our new consulting and technology business up and running. We were amazed by the BlackBerry 857 and 957 shown at a booth. We thought: "Wow—we can have access to read and reply to work email anywhere, anytime—that's fantastic!"

After we got back to Detroit, we purchased our first two BlackBerry smartphones. We even started peddaling them to our consulting clients. Selling them was great until our clients had a question or problem with their BlackBerry. It was at that point I began to realize that these things were addictive because of the severe pain they caused when they didn't work correctly. Which, fortunately, was rare.

> We were **hooked...**
> **Instant responses**
> to client email --
> **anywhere, anytime!**

We were hooked. Being a very small company that tried to be responsive to big clients, we used the devices to respond to all emails within a few minutes, rather than at the end of every day. It was great for both our clients and our growing business. We even got an lifestyle improvement. Instead of taking an extra 30 minutes at the end of every day to read and respond to email, we were "free." Or so we thought.

> We actually **believed**
> our Lifestyle had
> **improved!**

Then the symptoms began. First, it was a matter of checking the BlackBerry every time it buzzed and flashed: while watching TV, during family meals, in the car at stop lights, and eventually while driving on an "easy stretch of road."

My increased personal time started to morph into increased and never-ending work time. My family started to question and complain about my BlackBerry use. When I disappeared for a few minutes, my wife, Julie, would begin to ask: "Were you checking your BlackBerry?" I am a terrible liar, so I just had to confess immediately. I'd start to relish the times when I could check my BlackBerry without anyone else seeing my growing habit. Many times, the solitude of the bathroom was now "BlackBerry-time."

> I'd **relish** the times when I
> could '**steal away**' and
> check my BlackBerry

Once, to my great horror, I even dropped my BlackBerry right into the toilet. I snatched it out immediately, with little to no concern of what else was in there. I opened it right up and laid out the battery, battery cover, and SIM card on a paper towel. I gazed at my precious BlackBerry all opened up and spread across the counter in pieces. I almost felt as if I should draw white chalk lines around the pieces. Then, I started right away on resuscitating the waterlogged center of my universe. I began by trying to blow in all the holes, before breaking out the hair dryer out to try and salvage *my precious*.

Well, the CPR process worked, and the BlackBerry performed faithfully for another six months until it finally sputtered and died right in the middle of a phone call. I now had the perfect excuse to lay down some cash for the newest and greatest BlackBerry—thereby scoring another fix for my growing addiction.

I knew that I needed professional help, and I wondered if there were other users/abusers out there that might be able to benefit from my stories and those of other BlackBerry abusers. About that time, Gary and I hooked up with Kevin at www.CrackBerry.com, and we started laying the groundwork for this book. We gathered up lots of stories and other addiction avoidance tips, tricks, and strategies from the BlackBerry community and included the best of them in this short book. We hope you enjoy them and can benefit from our brief guide to overcoming BlackBerry addiction!

Introduction

We, the authors (Martin, Gary, and Kevin), sincerely thank you for taking the time to read this book on BlackBerry addiction. You may have purchased this book yourself or received it as a gift from a concerned colleague or loved one. However this guide came into your hands, we hope that we can help you make some small strides both toward becoming aware of your possible BlackBerry overuse and abuse, as well as in curbing those addictive BlackBerry behaviors you may have developed in your daily life.

TIP Do you know people addicted to their iPhone, Android, or other phones?

The smartphone landscape has continued to evolve in the two years since we wrote the first edition of this book. Now one could easily replace BlackBerry with iPhone or Android phones. While the stories and book are focused on BlackBerry smartphones, many of the same concepts will apply equally well regardless of type of phone you happen to be carrying around.

The BlackBerry is such a powerful and compelling tool that it can coax addictive or inappropriate behaviors out of even the most stalwart people. Our simple goal is that you become fully aware of your BlackBerry use, be much more sensitive to those around you, and in the end become a much more responsible BlackBerry user.

◼ CAUTION Constant Interruptions Can Hurt Your Brain's Abilities

Did you know that constant interruptions caused by your BlackBerry and other electronic devices can harm your ability to develop long-term memories and create new ideas? Loren Frank, a professor of physiology at the University of California, San Francisco, said downtime lets the brain go over experiences, "solidify them and turn them into permanent long-term memories."[1]

We hope that you begin to re-focus your attention away from the people on the other end of your BlackBerry to balance it with those people (friends, family and colleagues) that you can see and touch in your immediate vicinity.

> ## 59% of people Check Email from Bed with their Pajamas on.
> ### Source: AOL Email Addiction Survey

Many of us exhibit some addictive BlackBerry behaviors without even knowing it. We are so finely attuned to our BlackBerry that our attention can be instantaneously diverted by a quick buzz or flash of red light. Most times, we are not even aware that we are ignoring those around us, including those with whom we were speaking before the BlackBerry's interruption.

By no means do we advocate going "cold turkey," nor do we recommend getting rid of your precious 'Berry (there are many BlackBerry competitors out there, but there is only one BlackBerry!). We do, however, want you to develop an awareness of those bad habits and begin to employ some of our strategies to help you stop them. These habits can range from minor etiquette problems to actions that are very dangerous to yourself and others. Please take the stories to heart. Maybe you can identify with some of them, and thereby become more

---

[1] Source: "Digital Devices Deprive Brain of Needed Downtime" By Matt Richtel, Aug. 24, 2010, New York Times

aware of your own actions. More importantly, maybe you can take some small steps to improve your life with a BlackBerry.

> We feel better, more complete and more whole when we are tethered to our BlackBerry at all times.

Each of this book's authors has found a way to turn his love of his BlackBerry smartphone into his job. Kevin is a 110% BlackBerry-related worker, and Gary and Martin live on all sorts of technology – including their BlackBerrys pretty much all day long. All of us have a multitude of stories of BlackBerry use and abuse that we will share in the course of this book. We will also share the stories of many BlackBerry users; their stories will serve both as cautionary lessons and inspirational examples for curbing the more destructive aspects of BlackBerry overuse and abuse. This book is both a labor of love and a byproduct of three entrepreneurs who are admittedly addicted to their BlackBerry smartphones.

> ## 12% of People Check Email at Church.
>
> Source: AOL Email Addiction Survey

The Responsible BlackBerry User

We feel that it is important to say that BlackBerry smartphones can be—and are—extremely useful tools. They help us stay connected with colleagues, friends, and family; and they give us a freedom-of-movement and ease-of-use never before possible in a portable device. All BlackBerry devices today provide email, phone, BlackBerry Messenger (BBM), SMS text messaging, and web browsing out-of-the-box. They also include features such as cameras, GPS, and

WiFi, as well as support for powerful and popular apps such as Facebook, Twitter, Flikr, YouTube, and many more.

The BlackBerry frees us from sitting at our computer, enabling us to do many things that previously required us to be *tethered* to our desk. In many emerging markets, such as Indonesia and Venezuela, the availability of the Internet in homes is less prevalent. BlackBerry smartphone sales have skyrocketed in such cases, with the BlackBerry serving as an individual's main connection to the Internet. In other words, *the BlackBerry can be a very good—and even a great— thing!* It is precisely this high-degree of connectivity and usefulness that can lead some people to become compulsive in their use or abuse of the device.

Phantom Vibrations

I sometimes suffer from a case of phantom BlackBerry. That's when my BlackBerry is not on my belt, but I can still feel it vibrate as if it were receiving email. I reach down to check it... and it's not there! Am I losing it?

—*Paul C., MadeSimpleLearning.com Customer*

Unlike other habits that can morph into addiction, such as alcohol, drugs, and gambling, a BlackBerry habit does not have to become destructive to yourself or others. A heavy BlackBerry user can also be a responsible BlackBerry user. One of the main goals of this book is to help you become a more responsible BlackBerry user.

The Responsible BlackBerry User Credo:

I promise not to use my BlackBerry in any situation that could harm myself or others – either in body or mind.

Sometimes a BlackBerry user's abusive behavior can be characterized as a simple lack of good manners (e.g., ignoring others in a conversation); other times, it can be downright dangerous (e.g., crashing a car while using a BlackBerry). You will see examples at both ends of the spectrum of BlackBerry abuse in this book, as well as a few more in our "Chart of Shame" (see Figure 1).

CrackBerry Chart of Shame

Plain Rude

- Interrupt conversation to use your BlackBerry
- Read & respond to email during a meal with others
- Ignore your best friend to use your BlackBerry after work
- Ignore your spouse because you are using your BlackBerry
- Use BlackBerry while you are putting your child to sleep
- Use BlackBerry constantly while on vacation
- Talk loudly on BlackBerry in restaurant, library, movie, etc.
- Bumping into people because you are reading email while walking
- Ignoring traffic and pedestrians because you are using BlackBerry Messenger (BBM) while crossing the street
- Texting on BlackBerry while skiing on a crowded slope
- Type on BlackBerry while driving yourself
- Type on BlackBerry while driving with others in the vehicle

Downright Dangerous

Where do you stack up?

Figure 1. *The CrackBerry chart of shame.*

Early Days of the CrackBerry

The term *CrackBerry* has been used to define BlackBerry addicts since the early days of the device in the late 1990s; however, it's only in the last few years that the term has gone mainstream.

It's pretty **addictive**, that's why they call it **CrackBerry**

The degree to which many people now understand the term, both BlackBerry and non-BlackBerry users alike, reflects the strength of this BlackBerry addiction. The earliest citation of the term *CrackBerry* traces back to 2000 when Dennis Kavelman, the CFO of Research In Motion (the BlackBerry smartphone's manufacturer) was interviewed by Geoff Colvin from CNBC:

" Earliest Citation of the term "CrackBerry"

Kavelman: *"I'm not sure if you guys use BlackBerry or have tried it, but it is pretty addictive."*

Colvin: *"Well, it is addictive and on Wall Street they call it CrackBerry for exactly that reason. Once you try it you can't live without it, so they say."*
—From Research In Motion CFO Interview, CNBC, Sept. 29, 2000 "

BlackBerry users are passionate about their devices and willing to admit their dependence upon them.

" Benefits of BlackBerry Wireless Email

My BlackBerry enables me to prepare for the workday ahead. I know what kind of day I am going to have, and most days I will not log onto my computer much before 11:00am. The BlackBerry allows me this luxury.

—Alex W. "

CrackBerry Terms Defined

We were asked to define the word, so we came up with our own definition of the term CrackBerry:

CrackBerry

-n, *pl* –ries

informal slang, nickname for a BlackBerry smartphone that typically has a seductive flashing red light, vibration and satisfying keyboard that appears to have an addictive hold on many people who use it. People with a more severe addiction tend to ignore their immediate surroundings whenever the device vibrates or flashes, whether they are talking to someone, driving, walking or enjoying a meal with friends. Sometimes, people feel phantom vibrations This addictive nature can be controlled with a modified 12-step program found in the book *CrackBerry: True Tales of BlackBerry Use and Abuse.*

And below is a related term.

CrackBerry Prayer

-n, *pl* –s

informal slang, the act of trying to use your BlackBerry device by hiding it in one's lap, usually surreptitiously. The act looks somewhat like the individual is praying since they are holding the BlackBerry quietly in their lap, their hands are together (almost like praying), their shoulders are slightly hunched and their head is bowed to enable them to read the device.

If you have a question about some of the terms used in this book, please check out Appendix A: "CrackBerry Terms and Definitions" for a complete list of CrackBerry-related terms such as *push email, hard reset, BlackBerry Prayer,* and many more. If you don't see the information you're looking for, then you can always visit www.CrackBerry.com! Searching this site will often return a useful result to a question you're trying to answer or a problem you're trying to solve.

" I have been 2 minutes from work and realized my phone was on the counter at home and turned around and driven all the way back home to get it even though it meant being late for work. I'd much rather take my chances with my boss on being late than having to endure a whole workday without my BlackBerry!

—wolfpacker92, CrackBerry.com Member "

Presidential BlackBerry Addiction

Perhaps no single individual has done more for BlackBerry addiction recognition as our President, Barak Obama. His BlackBerry use (and abuse) was widely chronicled during the presidential campaign of 2008.

Also widely reported was his desire to keep his beloved BlackBerry once he took office.

Jeff Zeleny of the New York Times wrote;

> *"For years, like legions of other on-the-move professionals, Obama has been all but addicted to his BlackBerry. The device has rarely been far from his side - on most days, it was fastened to his belt - to provide a singular conduit to the outside world as the bubble around him grew tighter and tighter throughout his campaign."*[2]

In the end, the President was able to use a specially configured BlackBerry and can only email about 10 individuals in his inner circle – not quite what the BlackBerry addict was looking for, but, better than no BlackBerry at all!

BlackBerry Addiction Avoidance Tips

You will see many graphics like the one immediatley beneath this paragraph sprinkled throughout this book. Such graphics will contain tips and tricks to help wean you away from your addictive BlackBerry behaviors. You can find a complete list of BlackBerry Abuse Intervention and Etiquette Rules in Chapter 10: "BlackBerry Etiquette." The same chapter also includes some helpful BlackBerry Addiction Avoidance Tips.

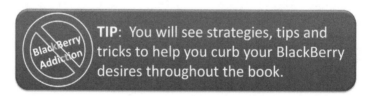

TIP: You will see strategies, tips and tricks to help you curb your BlackBerry desires throughout the book.

---

[2] http://www.nytimes.com/2008/11/16/world/americas/16iht-blackberry.1.17858157.html

> "I was screaming in pain and asked them to find my BlackBerry...my BlackBerry was ruined...The day I got out of the hospital, I went to buy a new BlackBerry"
>
> Source: Sue – Car Accident Survivor

Each of the authors has included his own stories related to BlackBerry use and addiction later in the this chapter. These stories will help you get a flavor for our background and experience with BlackBerry smartphone devices.

> How often do you look or check to make sure your BlackBerry is nearby?
> We all do it – it becomes our security blanket.

The Path to a BlackBerry 12 Step Program

The core of this book is structured in 12, easy-to-read chapters. Each chapter loosely mirrors the theme of the traditional 12 steps used by many addiction recovery programs today. You may notice some similarity and repetition between several chapters; this is intentional because we want to reinforce some of the key points and stay true to the spirit of the original 12 steps program, which also includes some degree of repetition. We give credit to the original 12 Steps that were published in the book, *Alcoholics Anonymous* in 1939[3].

We hope that you will take these 12 steps to heart. Some steps may be relatively easy for you, others may be quite difficult. It all depends on your personality,

---

[3] Source: *Alcoholics Anonymous* (June 2001). "Chapter 5: How It Works," 4th edition, Alcoholics Anonymous World Services.

level of awareness, personal desires, and above all else, the level of support and assistance you request and receive from those around you.

Our 12-Step CrackBerry Addiction Program

This book will walk you through our own 12-step program; together, these steps will help you overcome your BlackBerry addiction the negative consequences that result from it:

Step 1: Admit we are powerless without our BlackBerry.

Our lives have become unmanageable without our beloved 'Berrys. Like Pavlovian dogs, we have been slaves to the little red light, including its vibrations, rings and addictive keyboard.

Step 2: Believe in things more important than our BlackBerry.

While we may buy our BlackBerry gifts (think: BlackBerry cases, accessories, apps, games and themes) and sometimes engage in BlackBerry worship, we must connect with something else, such as those around us or a "higher power" to help restore our sanity.

Step 3: Begin to turn away from our BlackBerry abuse.

We resolve to begin occasionally turning our will and our lives over to the power of being BlackBerryless.

Step 4: Take a moral inventory of our BlackBerry abuses.

We create a general list of those times we behaved poorly or even in a way that was dangerous to those around us.

Step 5: Admit to our specific BlackBerry abuses.

We have taken the Addiction quiz and confessed to our specific list of BlackBerry abuses. We will share this confession with the universe, ourselves, and another human.

Step 6: Plan to be a more responsible BlackBerry user.

We commit to begin addressing our shortcomings and BlackBerry-related character defects.

Step 7: Ask for help in achieving responsible BlackBerry use.

We realize that we need help from those around us to become more responsible BlackBerry users. This might mean having others put our BlackBerry in safe place until we can learn to use it without hurting ourselves or others.

Step 8: List those BlackBerry bystanders we have wronged.

We will make a list of all those people (named and unnamed) that we have hurt because of our BlackBerry addiction.

Step 9: Make amends to our BlackBerry bystanders.

We will make amends to those whom we have wronged with our BlackBerry abuses; we will "Scoop our BlackBerry Poop."

Step 10: Adhere tirelessly to BlackBerry etiquette rules.

We resolve to live by the BlackBerry Etiquette Rules. When we break them, we will work hard to fix our ways.

Step 11: Resolve to reconnect with others around us.

We resolve to reconnect and have *conscious contact* with those directly around us, rather than *constant contact* with those on the other end of our BlackBerry.

Step 12: Resolve to be responsible and spread the word.

We resolve to stick to the rules and help other BlackBerry abusers learn and practice these rules of responsible BlackBerry Use. We promise to "Type the Talk" and "Walk the Walk." We encourage everyone we know to buy this book and learn the path to responsible BlackBerry use.

You may notice that our 12 chapters do not follow the original 12 steps exactly; however, we do try to be conscious of the original 12 steps as our guiding principles. Some of the verbiage and stories are clearly tongue-in-cheek. Nevertheless, we strongly believe there are serious issues raised that many of us can relate to. Unfettered BlackBerry overuse can cause problems in our relationships, in our careers, and in our social interaction. The stories contained within this book and the analysis and suggestions of the authors will, we hope, help you on chart a path to safe and responsible BlackBerry use.

"I Can't Be Without It!"

In this chapter, we'll cover the first step to overcoming BlackBerry addiction: admitting we have a problem.

We are ruled by the little
RED blinking light!

Step 1:
Admit We Are Powerless
Without Our BlackBerry

Step 1: Admit we are powerless without our BlackBerry. Our lives have become unmanageable without our beloved 'Berrys. Like Pavlovian dogs, we are slaves to the little red light, including its vibrations and rings.

In other words, the first step in beginning to overcome our addiction is to stop and think about the way that the BlackBerry interferes with our lives and to admit that we are powerless over its pull.

Consider this common experience. We put our BlackBerry smartphone down beside our computer and type away. Every few seconds, however, we find ourselves looking to the side. "Did we just see the red light blink?" We wonder. We pick it up to take a closer look. No, no light, so back to work we go. We repeat this process every few minutes. "Did my friend reply to my BBM yet?" "Maybe I should PING him!" "I love typing and feel the clickety clack of the keyboard!"

We could swear that we saw that light go off. More often than not, we are mistaken.

> **I was lost when my BlackBerry was lost... Once located, I made a vow — never to lose *my companion* again.**
>
> **Source: Steve – BlackBerry Abuser**

What does this say about us? Well, it says that we might very well be addicted to our BlackBerry. It isn't just the light we look for. When we have our BlackBerry holstered or in **Vibrate** mode, we are certain we can feel our little buddy shake on our belt. Often, we are mistaken. These phantom vibrations are a little bit spooky, and they speak to our continual attachment to our BlackBerry device. That same attachment led the authors to sit down and write this book.

`` Must...Check...Messages Now!

Who waits 30 minutes to check their BlackBerry? Not me. It's a Pavlovian response. The bell goes off to indicate a message. I walk like Frankenstein across the room, arms out— "must... check... messages..."

If someone writes me, I must immediately see what that person wants or needs. I try to turn my BlackBerry off on weekends and at night, but what if someone needs something?

Anyone else ever forget to "go" when the traffic light turns green because they're busy reading or writing messages?

—Karen L. ``

An International Problem

The problem seems to transcend the shores of North America—it is a world-wide problem. In August of 2010, Saudi Arabia's telecom operator CITC announced a ban on BlackBerry services due to security concerns. (The argument was that the BlackBerry security system was too good to be broken by the government so it might be used by criminals without detection.)

This has been met with resistence and a fair bit of anger from BlackBerry Addicts in the Middle East.

`` Reaction to Proposed BlackBerry Ban

I understand that there is a security issue and that's why it's being banned," says Manal Sanai, "But it's really going to affect my social life. I spend hours BBMing [BlackBerry Messaging] my friends. There is only one person in my class who doesn't have one and if you don't have one then you are kind of left behind.

—Manal Sanai, a self-confessed BlackBerry addict[1] ``

---

[1] http://worldblog.msnbc.msn.com/_news/2010/08/06/4831595-uae-blackberry-ban-curbing-terrorism-or-curbing-flirting

The Roots of the Problem

So, what is it about our BlackBerry smartphone that has us continually checking to see whether the light is going off or if the device is vibrating, even when it isn't? There are no single, simple answer for this—many reasons exist for our attachment and addiction to our BlackBerry.

That said, there are a few key reasons that help to make us feel powerless over the BlackBerry's pull:

We're always connected: We live in a world where we believe we must always be connected *to friends, family and colleagues.*

Communication feels good: We like hearing from people, whether it's through email, text messages, pictures, or some other method. Receiving communication from others makes us feel good.

Checking messages make us feel important: It gives us a sense of increased self importance to have messages that require a response, especially if we know others can see us using our BlackBerry.

We're Always Connected

The freedom to be anywhere—whether it's a grocery store, a sporting event, golf course, pool, or anywhere else—and still instantly read and respond to important email or other message as if we were sitting at our desk.

One potential reason for this need to continually check the flashing red light is that this is expectations we have set for responding quickly, anytime of the day or night. We are continually connected with our BlackBerry smartphones. We know it, and, everyone who knows us, knows it as well. We have created the situation—nobody else did this to us—and that's important to remember. We use the BlackBerry, and we respond to the messages as soon as they arrive.

Most of us hate to disappoint people, especially those we care about. This holds true for both our professional and personal contacts. If people want our attention, we want to be there for them. Our BlackBerry smartphones allow and encourage this behavior. The problem is that this becomes a self-perpetuating problem. If we create a world in which we are always *accessible*, we are never *off.*

Communication Feels Good

The second reason for our bad behavior of continually checking for that little red light is that we like hearing from people. It feels good to have business associates, colleagues, friends, and family reach out to us.

When Gary was a kid, he would run to the mailbox as soon as the mail carrier would drop off the mail (OK, sometimes he still does this!). "Did anyone write to me today?" Gary would wonder to himself. When a letter came, there was great joy—even if the person who wrote wasn't someone he was particularly fond of. If nothing came, he felt disappointed.

When the light blinks, someone is communicating with us: we are not alone. Our BlackBerry smartphones bring us instant gratification by letting us know the instant someone wants us.

Tip Replying Quickly to Email can Be Addictive.

"According to scientists, juggling e-mail, phone calls and other incoming information ... play to a primitive impulse to respond to immediate opportunities and threats. This stimulation provokes excitement – a dopamine squirt – that researchers say can be addictive. In its absence, people feel bored."[2]

---

[2] Source: "Attached to Technology and Paying a Price" by Matt Richtel, June 6, 2010, New York Times.

❝ Can't Leave Home Without It

I recently had just driven one hour of a four-hour trip when I realized I had left my BlackBerry on the kitchen counter. I turned around and went back to get it without a second thought!

—Oscar M., MadeSimpleLearning.com Customer

Checking Messages Makes Us Feel Important

The third reason for continually checking that little light is perhaps the least flattering, but perhaps the most telling, if we're honest: it makes us feel important. Have you ever found yourself sitting in the airport, on a bus or train, and the first thing you do is take out your BlackBerry to check email? What do you do if nothing is there? Do you pretend that you are doing something important? Do you do something—anything— to make it *seem* as though you are a *somebody* who needs to be continually connected?

TIP: When you arrive home, check your BlackBerry at the door and <u>do not look at it until after dinner</u>.

What fuels this need of ours? Well, there are lots of explanations, many of which are as diverse as our population. Freud would bring this all back to a discussion about our *ego* and *id*. The Dalai Lama would tie this into our desire to be happy. Feeling important gives us a sense of purpose, which in turn makes us feel useful and happy.

❝ He Couldn't Be Without It

I was dating a man who had both a BlackBerry and phone. He lives in another state. When he would travel to town on business, he always had his "BlackBerry on Board."

We had been talking in a restaurant and, mid-sentence, he would reach for the vibration and start typing furiously with thumbs that shouldn't be able to move that quickly.

Once at the hotel, he would immediately plug it in and put it on a wood surface so that he could hear it without changing the ringer. It was the last thing he checked before turning in for the night and the first thing he checked in the morning after getting his glasses. If we left the room to go swimming, it was the first thing he looked at when returning to the room.

—J. K. ❞

For many years, BlackBerry smartphones were the property of the higher- ups in the business and government world, the *suits* or execs. Those early adopters always looked so darn important checking email, typing with their thumbs, and we wanted to be like them and have what they had. In recent years, the explosion of BlackBerry smartphones has allowed many more people, even us "non-higher-ups," to get in on the BlackBerry world. Some of us like to display our BlackBerry proudly on our belt, which might be telling the world: "I am important."

Often, what is behind our own feeling of self-importance is really our own insecurity. We look for validation from others to say: "That person is really important!" We need to remember this quote:

> *"We are so vain that we even care for the opinion of those we don't care for."*
>
> — *Marie Von Ebner-Eschenbach*
> *(Austrian novelist, 1830-1916.)*

Truth be told, checking our BlackBerry constantly doesn't make us look *important*. It makes us look like a Geek who checks his or her BlackBerry too much!

Why the BlackBerry is So Addictive

A research study conducted by MIT reported that almost all (90%) of BlackBerry users in one company felt a compulsion to use their BlackBerry. You can find that research study written up at this URL:

www.cio.com/article/29081/Management_Report_BlackBerry_Addiction_
Starts_at_the_Top

Such compulsion is characterized by a difficulty in refraining from checking the device at regular intervals. It is interesting, but not surprising, that compulsive behavior (i.e., CrackBerry addiction) affects an epidemic proportion of BlackBerry smartphone users. However, it is surprising that few users can offer substantive reasons why they feel compelled to constantly check their device. *Sure, they know they are doing it, but they do not stop to think about it, nor do they realize why.*

❝ BlackBerry On Bike

I have rigged up my bike so that I can see my BlackBerry screen while I'm riding. My local superstore sells a package of black Velcro Fashion Trim—it comes four strips in a package. They are one inch by three feet. I cut about one foot off and wrapped it around the main bar. I leave the last three to four turns with a slight loop in them. These last three to four loops were not pulled tightly around the ones underneath it. This leaves a space that allows me to clip my BlackBerry holster belt clip through it. Another strip can be wrapped around the lower part of the BlackBerry and around the bar to secure it a little better...I do this whenever I ride.

—Lenny M., MadeSimpleLearning.com Customer ❞

The three reasons we have proposed so far for "checking the little red light" have been largely psychological in nature. We are continually connected, we like to hear from people, and we like to feel important. If this were solely the case, it only makes sense that we should see all smartphones get an equal share of the blame for this gadget addiction phenomena, rather than just BlackBerry smartphones. And we do in fact see stories of addiction related to mobile gadgets other than the BlackBerry. However, there is something about the BlackBerry that arguably elicits more or this addictive compulsive behavior than occurs with other smartphone on the market.

66 Eat, Sleep, and Dream BlackBerry

I am afraid that I am really addicted to my BlackBerry. I manage the BlackBerry for my group, approximately 20 people. I eat, sleep and dream BlackBerry. I never shut mine off; it is on 24/7. And even when I get up in the middle of the night, the first thing I do is check my BlackBerry. I have had three models and I'm waiting for the new one to come out. I take my BlackBerry everywhere with me. Around here, I am known as the "BlackBerry Guru." Thanks for listening.

—Patricia M., MadeSimpleLearning.com Customer

It is often said the best way to sell a BlackBerry is to give one to someone to use for a week. In other words, give them a *taste*. The BlackBerry is a tangible device, and RIM, more than any other manufacturer on the market, has hit the key physical ingredients that we believe give the BlackBerry its psychological *CrackBerry* reputation: *Always On, Always Connected.*

▨ **Note** RIM has even registered the "Always On, Always Connected" phrase as a trademark with the US Patent and Trademark office.

You don't ever really turn your BlackBerry off. Once it boots up, it can run for months without ever having to be fully-powered off.

▨ **Note** Even the pressing the **Power** key does not really turn off the device; rather, it puts the device into a **Sleep** mode, so it can be instantly brought back to life by a single touch of the same **Power** key.

Pull a BlackBerry out of its holster, and the display is on. Drop it into its holster, and the display turns off. If you have it sitting beside you on the desk, and you see the red message notification light flashing, then you can hit any button, and the display will power up. This makes the BlackBerry extremely accessible. You never have to wait for it—it's always ready for use.

𝟔𝟔 Cannot Resist—Busted!

One night I was sitting in my living room reading a book. My BlackBerry was in its cradle in the kitchen, and my NASCAR alerts kept going off. I looked at my wife, and she looked at me and then I went back to reading my book. It kept on going off and I was dying.

She said, "Are you going to answer that?" I said, "Nah... it's no big deal." Then my wife got up and left the room. I sat there for another minute or two, and finally I couldn't stand it.

I went to the kitchen, grabbed my BlackBerry, and started reading my alerts. I turned around, and when I did, my wife was standing right there with a big ole grin. I was busted!

—Ed H. 𝟗𝟗

It's a One-Handed Device

The BlackBerry has always been very much a one-handed device. While most users take a two-handed, two-thumbed "crackberry prayer" approach for typing out emails, basic use of the phone (navigation, using applications, and so on) is easily accomplished with one hand. With a trackball or trackpad in the middle of the phone, the **Menu** key to the left, and **Escape/Back** button to the right, you don't need to move your thumb more than a half inch in any direction to have complete use of the phone. The same can't be said for most of the other smartphones on the market today. The iPhone and Android phones require the use of two hands that move much farther than one-half inch, as do most other devices that rely on a touch screen. Because the BlackBerry is so easy to use one-handed, people are tempted to use it anywhere and everywhere.

You can "get away" with using it during meetings, functions, and class because all that's required is one eye on the screen and a little bit of thumb movement. It can be an inconspicuous device when you need it to be. Unfortunately, this one-handed ease-of-use also means that people use their BlackBerry while driving. (The authors strenuously recommend that you do not use your BlackBerry while driving any vehicle, watercraft, or aircraft.)

> # 37% of People Check Email While They Drive.
>
> ### Source: AOL Email Addiction Survey

A growing number of US states are banning texting (sending text messages on your cell phones) while driving, and many articles you read about these bans will mention the BlackBerry somewhere in them.

Instant Communication

The BlackBerry has been designed to be the fastest communication tool. As such, it is second to no other device. We are all familiar with RIM's *push* email technology, and it's a given that the BlackBerry is quick to receive emails. More than that, it's the speed with which a BlackBerry can be used to reply to that newly received message or send communication (e.g., email, text message, PIN message, or place a phone call) that is really impressive.

Did you receive an email and need to respond? Pull your BlackBerry out of its holster and it will automatically turn on the display, open the email application, and display the new message. Zero clicks and no time wasted. Compare this to an iPhone, where you would have to power on, slide to unlock, tap once to open the email application, and tap again to view the inbox and the newly received message. We are talking about 15 seconds taken before you can even view the message received in the first place. If you observe BlackBerry users, you'll notice they reach for the devices many, many times during the course of a day, but each interaction with the device is quite short. This isn't a coincidence, but by design. Research in Motion's philosophy is for the BlackBerry to be an on-the-go device. Studies have shown that you can literally add about an hour of productivity to your day by utilizing all of brief moments of downtime you have between activities.

It Calls to You

The blinking red light is *addictive*. You can turn it off, but nobody does. The blinking red light lets you know you have a new message of some sort waiting, whether it's an email, missed call, text, PIN, or chat program message. Beyond the red light, you can customize your notification profiles for your BlackBerry. For example, you can make the phone vibrate when you receive a message when the device is in its holster or case. It's hard to ignore the vibrations and blinks of a BlackBerry, especially when you can check your message so quickly.

The BlackBerry has *crazy long battery life*. You'll rarely hear a BlackBerry user complain about battery life. The original BlackBerry 857/957 could run for two weeks or more without a charge, and the 72xx Series BlackBerry smartphones could literally run for days and days on a single charge. The newer BlackBerry models don't have quite the same battery life; however, compared to other phones on the market, even the current devices are marathon runners. This means the BlackBerry can be relied on. You always know it's going to be there, even at the end of the day or late at night—whenever you need it.

" Jet Ski and Fender Benders

I have three BlackBerry smartphones in the bottom of Wolf Lake, and that's not three berries that you might eat, that's telephones from falling out of my Jet Ski. They're gone. One of the most memorable experiences I have had was a fender bender with my Dodge pickup truck when trying to read the BlackBerry menu. I totaled one woman's poor Sunbird car on a wet pavement day.

I have your book: "BlackBerry Made Simple" on my desktop, a self-help book downloaded off the Internet because the local cell phone dealership cannot answer my more difficult or advanced questions.

—Duane S., MadeSimpleLearning.com Customer "

The Clikety-Clack of the Keyboard

There is something satisfying about typing on the keyboard. The feel of the keys under our fingers, it gives us the sense of getting something done.

Last, but certainly not least to mention is the famous BlackBerry keyboard. In a competitive smartphone marketplace where the current trend is toward big touchscreen devices, the physical keyboard is not only one of the key visible attributes that identifies a BlackBerry, but it's one of the single biggest reasons people buy a BlackBerry and can't give up their BlackBerry.

In a recent poll on CrackBerry.com with over 20,000 respondents, 43% said they'll *never* give up having a physical keyboard on their smartphone. Another 35% said they much prefer having a physical keyboard compared to typing on glass. While there are BlackBerry device models that are full touchscreen, the physical keyboard has been a RIM staple prior to even BlackBerry being on the market.

Just recently RIM has introduced it's first touch screen BlackBerry with a slide out keyboard, the Torch 9800. It's hard to get away from the keyboard – people love them so much and truly identify a BlackBerry by its keyboard.

In the late 90s, the BlackBerry bucked the touchscreen trend already in use by devices like the Palm Pilot. While Palm was trying to perfect their stylus-based Graffiti method of data input, which converted handwriting into text, the RIM keyboard almost appeared to be a step backwards.

Appearance and usage are different things, though, the full physical QWERTY keyboard was immediately embraced by anybody who picked up the device. Despite the small size of the buttons, typing on a physical keyboard proved easy and the tactile feedback of pushing buttons allowed for faster more accurate typing. It also allowed the user to build up muscle memory – just like typing on a computer keyboard after a while you don't have to think about where the keys are.

The success of the RIM/BlackBerry keyboard was so overwhelming that it even forced Palm to release a device featuring a full physical keyboard. Thanks to the speed and ease of typing provided by the BlackBerry keyboard, the ability to pound out a reply to a message so quickly has people doing just that -- anytime and everywhere – which unfortunately leads to BlackBerry Addiction.

The Addiction

No addiction starts overnight. It takes at least some time to form, although it's surprising just how fast BlackBerry addiction can creep up. In the case of Vanessa, she was well aware of the BlackBerry smartphone's addictive tendencies before she ever held one. One might think that this foresight would allow her to avoid the uncontrollable urge to reach for her BlackBerry. As "Vanessa's Story" shows us, sometimes rational knowledge is useless when it comes to the irresistible draw of the BlackBerry.

66 Vanessa's Story

My name is Vanessa and I'm a CrackBerry addict. Years ago I experienced what a lot of spouses are only experiencing now. My husband was one of the "pioneers" of BlackBerry addiction. I couldn't understand his obsession with this phone. Most of all, I couldn't understand what was so fascinating about a bulky phone with tiny, almost impossible-to-type keys. It was like he had just had a baby and all he could talk about and read about was BlackBerry. BlackBerry this, BlackBerry that!

He would make up a reason to go out, just so he could check his email without having his laptop in front of him. We would be out to dinner, and he would be constantly checking his email. If he wasn't checking his email, he was telling me all about the great features of his device. Not exactly the best date you could have.

All I wanted was to have a nice dinner with a real conversation that didn't involve him typing or spinning a wheel. This black box was really getting on my nerves!

Last year we had this really long drive, 12 hours in a car. My husband started the drive. At the beginning there was music and conversation, and then I realized the clock on the dashboard was broken. Oh no, my watch was broken too! Alas, actually we were both dying of boredom, and time seemed to be running in slow motion. That was when I first noticed that little light from the BlackBerry blinking at me. It kept calling my name and telling me: try me... try me... And just like that, my hands were wrapped around my biggest enemy of all time. And I started to become friends with my former nemesis.

After a couple of minutes, I had figured out its powers, and I was on a roll! I was the queen of the World Wide Web. I was reading emails, sending emails, checking up on the weather, and looking at Google Maps. I didn't want to let go of my new little friend. Meanwhile my husband kept saying that it was my turn to drive. But I knew that what he really meant was that it was his turn to use the BlackBerry.

At the beginning of this year, I was on the phone with one of my best friends. She lives in Germany, and her husband had just started a new job and was awarded a BlackBerry. She complained how he kept staring at it all the time, how he couldn't disconnect from it, and how he kept sending replies to his boss at 11pm on a Saturday night. It's like the BlackBerry had become his mistress, and there was no space for her in his new world. And I had the most unexpected behavior. I started to defend him! And then it hit me! I had become one of them; I was a CrackBerry addict!

—Vanessa, CrackBerry.com Member

Vanessa's story is *not* unique. The world is quickly becoming a country of email addicts. In the second quarter of 2010, the worldwide smartphone market grew at a 64 percent annual rate. RIM's shipment of BlackBerry smartphones grew at a rate of 41 percent annually. And this is all happening during a global economic slow down. There has to be something with these smartphones!

Canalys estimates, http://www.canalys.com/pr/2010/r2010081.html

An AOL survey discovered the extent to which we have made 24/7 access to email a must-have in our lives. While AOL's survey is not exclusively about BlackBerry smartphones, at the time of the survey in 2008, the BlackBerry was the best known wireless email device.

According to AOL's third annual Email Addiction survey[3], more Americans than ever before are using portable devices to keep tabs on their email throughout the day and night, and from virtually anywhere—from their bed, cars, bathrooms, and even church.

83% of email users check their email on vacation, and increasing number of people plan the location of their getaways based on Internet access and wireless BlackBerry coverage.

Some other statistics from the email survey are quite telling:

- 59% of people emailing from portable devices are checking email in bed while in their pajamas.
- 37% are checking email while they drive.
- 12% admit to checking email in church.

Visit any of the popular BlackBerry community websites, and you will discover so many of the tens of thousands of active BlackBerry users who frequent them that these statistics could well be understating things. CrackBerry.com just passed the 2.5 million member mark in mid-2010. A phenominal growth rate in just a few short years.

91% of People Check Email in the Bathroom.

Source: CrackBerry.com Poll

---

[3] Source: AOL.com: http://o.aolcdn.com/cdn.webmail.aol.com/survey/aol/en-us/index.htm

In a poll at www.CrackBerry.com, more than 91% of respondents indicated they use their BlackBerry in the bathroom. Many respondents included comments like this one: "I think someone would be lying if they said they don't take it with them!"

About **100 damaged** BlackBerry Smartphones received every week have been **dropped in the toilet**

"Oh... s--t!"

Many, many BlackBerry users even bring their device into the bathroom with them, often with catastrophic consequences. David Van Tongerloo, vice president of "The BlackBerry Repair Shop" in Houston, said that about 100 of the 500 damaged devices he receives a week have been dropped in the toilet. "We wear rubber gloves and masks when handling these devices," he said. "We only do that for BlackBerry smartphones that were dropped in the toilet."[4]

---

[4] Source: http://jscms.jrn.columbia.edu/cns/2008-04-15/mamdani-blackberry

> ## "We wear rubber gloves and masks to handle BlackBerrys dropped in the toilet."
>
> Source: David Van Tongerloo, "The BlackBerry Repair Shop"

Reading the news on a BlackBerry in the bathroom has its benefits, according to Stephen Sodoris, a professor of social work at the University of Maryland. "The BlackBerry is a distraction technique for the millions of people who have a *shy-bladder* or fear of going to the bathroom in public," he said.

Some BlackBerry owners are so reluctant to be without the device that they will do almost anything to ensure they don't have to ever part ways with it (see the story, "BlackBerry During a Funeral").

## 	" BlackBerry During a Funeral

I recently dove deep into the ocean to retrieve my BlackBerry after dropping it while fishing. Later, I stopped to look for it after my infant daughter tossed it out of my car window on a freeway! My love for my BlackBerry means I will do just about anything to protect it, but also that I will use it anywhere I please, including the time I stood at my father-in-law's funeral, felt my BlackBerry vibrating in my pocket, and the urge was too powerful to resist. Not only did I scroll through my new messages during the service, but I responded, too. My addiction stems from an obsession with reading and responding to email as soon as it arrives.

—John, CrackBerry.com Member 	"

While BlackBerry addiction can cause all sorts of nuisances in a social context, it becomes a greater concern when it puts people's lives at risk, such as when using your BlackBerry while driving (see Bell's story in "Mercedes Crashed by BlackBerry." Bell's accident occurred after only a single week with the device!

66 BlackBerry Caused Mercedes Crash

I have had my BlackBerry about a week, and have already had my first accident with it. I was driving and checking an email that just came in (stupid I know!) and ran my fiancé's Mercedes into the car in front of me. I have not admitted to being on my phone at the time of the crash, but he knows. I guess that was my initiation.

—Bell, CrackBerry.com Member **99**

Nobody was injured in this instance, and Bell says she has learned her lesson and will never use her BlackBerry while driving again. But using the BlackBerry when driving is a sure sign of the BlackBerry smartphone's addictive grasp. An even stronger portrayal of BlackBerry addiction is painted by Sue's recent recollection of a severe car accident, where the one thing on her mind wasn't the physical condition of her husband or herself, but the location and condition of their BlackBerry smartphone (see the story, "We Hit a Stopped Truck at 60 MPH").

❝ We Hit a Stopped Truck at 60 mph

On February 1st, 2008, I proudly walked out of the AT&T store after upgrading my Pearl to a Curve 8310. The next day, my husband and I were traveling out of town. Since he was driving, I used the time to set up my Curve. My Curve was in my hand, and my old Pearl, my husband's Curve (which I had just bought him in December), and my BlackBerry 7290 (issued by my employer) were all in my lap.

We were using TeleNav on my Curve for directions and were cruising down the road when I glanced up from my Curve to see a truck stopped in front of us. My husband yelled as we hit it at 60mph, flipped three times then slid upside down on the roof before stopping. We were upside down when we stopped moving, hanging by our seatbelts. When we were taken out of the car, I was in severe pain.

As we were waiting to be air-lifted, people were gathering our personal belongings. I was screaming in pain and asked them to find my BlackBerry. And they brought one, and then another, and then another until they located all of them. I can't imagine what they thought. When we arrived at the trauma unit, my left hand was black. They asked what was I doing when we crashed. My family all responded: "Holding her BlackBerry!" (I had lost three units of blood internally and am still recovering.)

All our BlackBerry smartphones were ruined. The day I got out of the hospital, I went to AT&T to get new Curves. Since there was no insurance on them and we had just signed new two-year contracts, I could not get either of our BlackBerry smartphones replaced without paying full price. Even being on pain pills did not help the pain of losing my precious Curve. Since I could do nothing but lie in bed, I started calling AT&T daily, trying to get someone to help me. It was pure torture to be without my Curve by my side. Finally, one day I reached someone who said, "I can get you two Curves for $99 each and a $100 rebate if you agree to another two-year contract." That was not a problem; for that price, I would have signed away my next grandchild! (Not really, but I would have considered it — briefly.) My Curve is once again forever by my side.

—Sue 🙶

"Do I Worship My BlackBerry?"

In this chapter, we'll walk you through the second step in overcoming your BlackBerry addiction: admitting there are more important things in life than our BlackBerry.

There really are things more important than that little smartphone from Canada. Sometimes we just get caught up in our texting, emailing, BlackBerry Messenging, and checking facebook, so much that we lose sight of what is really important around us.

In this chapter we will look at the dangers of worshiping our BlackBerry and try to shift focus onto those things in our lives that are even more important than the BlackBerry.

The "BlackBerry Prayer"
Head bent down slightly, reverently, hands in lap, silently typing away. Quiet, focused, ignoring everything around us.

Step 2:
Believe in Things More Important Than Our BlackBerry

Step 2: Believe in things more important than our BlackBerry. While we may buy our BlackBerry gifts (think: BlackBerry cases, accessories, apps, games and themes) and sometimes engage in BlackBerry worship, we must connect with something, such as those around us or a "higher power" to help restore our sanity.

In other words, the second step in beginning to overcome our addiction is to begin to admit that there are things more important in life than our BlackBerry.

The second step in the path to recovery is usually acknowledged to be the realization that there is something that we define as our "higher power." For many, it is a belief in God. For others, it transcends the traditional notion of a deity or is even more obtuse. For too many of us, this step on the journey requires us to take a *leap of faith* that we are unwilling to commit to.

" Almost Hit by Bus for BlackBerry

I was walking across a busy city street during lunchtime and dropped my BlackBerry. Yes, I dashed out and picked it up, without thinking. I swear that Metro bus just missed me!

—Chandra N. "

For BlackBerry users and abusers, the issue is both crystal clear and intensely complicated at the same time: we worship our BlackBerry smartphones. And we demonstrate our worship of these little messaging devices in several ways:

- We pay complete attention to our BlackBerry, sometimes ignoring everything and everyone else around us.

- We show them adoration and shower them with gifts.

- We long for them and feel more "complete" when they are by our side.

- We ask things of them—sometimes, we even beg them to help us.

We like to think of ourselves as people who love human beings. We might say: "I love my spouse and my kids and my family and friends. I love time spent with those who are important to me. I hate to admit it, but *I also love my BlackBerry.*"

We, the authors, really love these devices. And my guess is, so do most of you reading this book. Why do we have such adoration for this small hunk of metal, plastic, and computer components? We love it for all the things we believe it does for us. There is no truer indication of this than the fact we turn to our BlackBerry when we are in need:

- When we need to reach out and communicate in a hurry – to whom or what do we turn? *To our BlackBerry.*

- When we need to find out the weather in Chicago before we get on the plane, where do we turn? *To our BlackBerry.*

- When we need to know how the Red Sox are doing, where do we turn? *You know where.*

> # We turn to our
> ## BlackBerry when we
> ## are in need.

We must check email, enter text, or search for something on our BlackBerry at least 50 times a day. It is the crutch upon which we lean for many things that we deem to be important.

How do we show adoration for those things that we rely on? One way is to shower them with gifts. In Biblical times, the ancient Israelites offered sacrifices to their God. As history moved on, sacrifices were replaced by prayer and other offerings still in use today. It is human nature to bestow gifts upon those we love and, yes, upon those we worship.

> ## I have 5 cases to protect
> ## my BlackBerry from the
> ## cruel world.

Gary muses about how he protects his BlackBerry:

> My BlackBerry can be protected from the horrors of our cruel world by one of no less than five protective cases I've purchased for it. I didn't purchase these protective devices for me—I bought them for my BlackBerry, to care for it. I can dress it up in leather if I take it out on the town, and I can protect it in armor if I need to risk its very being out in the world. If I go to the beach, it can be sealed in a hardened, plastic, waterproof case, so no harm befalls it.

> Also, I want it to look good at all times, so I "dress it up" with themes, wallpaper, and other things. I buy these things so it can look its best. I know that my BlackBerry doesn't want to look like everyone else's. Mine craves a sense of style and individuality! It communicates with me on that very deep level, so I take care of its every need.

Like all things we worship, we enter into a bargaining agreement with our BlackBerry. The healthier relationships between humanity and the higher power look at *covenantal* relationships (contracts between the parties); these contracts express obligations and expectations. So, I provide for and take care of my BlackBerry. In return, it will always be there for me. It will fetch my email when I want it, connect and not drop calls, keep my data safe, entertain me when I am lonely, and always wink at me with affection when my email comes in.

> I provide for and take care of my BlackBerry and it will always be there for me.

The second way we show that we show we worship our BlackBerry devices: We long for them and feel more complete when our device is by our side. Gary's good friend Steve recently converted to using a BlackBerry instead of a Windows Mobile phone. He has quickly become, not only a BlackBerry user, but also a BlackBerry abuser—so much so that he went into a panic last year when he couldn't find his new best friend.

He was lost when his BlackBerry was lost—incomplete until it was once again by his side. Indeed, he did what any good BlackBerry user and abuser would do: he went online and purchased a BlackBerry locator program. Once he located it, he made a vow that he would never lose his companion again.

> Getting Dressed Checklist:
> Wallet, check.
> Keys, check.
> BlackBerry, check.

How many times have we walked out of our homes and offices, jumped into our cars, and then realized that we left our BlackBerry behind, alone, to face the challenges of the world unprotected by us, its caretaker. What do most of us do when this happens? Kevin states: "I know that, when this has happened to me (and I am ashamed to admit it has happened more than once), I have run right back to where I was to retrieve my BlackBerry. I owe my device that much, at least."

" Driving 30 Minutes to Retrieve My BlackBerry

I'm in trouble here, just cant get enough! Just today I realized, when I was at my desk I forgot my phone at home. I quickly decided to leave work and drive the 30 minutes to get home to get it.

Before my BlackBerry, I never would have done that, I would have used my office phone, or emailed from my computer to tell friends that I'm sans phone. Nope, not now, I went all the way home to get my BlackBerry.

—Coolguy78240, CrackBerry.com Member "

How often do you check to make sure your BlackBerry is nearby? How many times do you feel your belt or pocket or purse, even when you know you have your BlackBerry with you? We all do it; it becomes our security blanket.

There are many reasons why our BlackBerry gives us a sense of security; we spoke of some of these in Chapter 1. Whatever the reason, the driving force is the same. We feel better and more complete when we are tethered to our BlackBerry at all times. And we do mean at **all** times. Later in this book, we will look at stories and situations where keeping your BlackBerry by your side everywhere you go can lead to disaster.

The third way we show that we worship our BlackBerry is that we ask things of it. For example, sometimes we beg our BlackBerry to help us. Have you ever caught yourself talking to your BlackBerry? "Come on, please! Don't crap out on me now! Please connect… please connect." Or perhaps you have said: "Just this one time. I have to send this email. Just give me a connection for a couple of seconds, and I won't ask anything more of you."

No doubt you have also seen the following on the train, in the airport, or at lunch. Frantic people (executives, young people, middle-aged people, anyone) will shake the BlackBerry, and curse, pray, and beg for the hour glass to disappear or for the connection to get magically stronger.

And what happens when our prayers are answered? Smiles, tears, and praises of thanksgiving.

We have all said, "Thank you, Thank you!" on more than one occasion when our BlackBerry finally did what we begged of it. We don't really stop to imagine what a non-BlackBerry user might think of one of us in that situation.

> **Worshiping** our BlackBerry is truly a sign of our **dependency**.

This behavior, this worship of our devices, is truly a sign of our *dependency*. We need to see this for what it is, and we need to acknowledge that it exists. Only when we take the steps of admitting our behavior and acknowledging that we do sometimes worship our BlackBerry can we begin to walk along the path towards becoming untethered, thereby freeing ourselves up for the things that are truly more important in our lives (see the story, "Worshiping My BlackBerry Is Caused by My Obsession with People").

" Worshiping My BlackBerry Is Caused by My Obsession with People

Hmm, I'm scared to even post my story because I'd like to think of myself as somewhat "normal", and by sharing my feelings towards my BlackBerry publicly will only save them for posterity. But here goes... (I figure that if even one person out there nods her head when reading my story, with a deep feeling of empathy and understanding, then posting is worth it!)

It's not that I have one instance of obsession. But every minute of every waking hour seems to be some homage to my addiction. Let's see... do others find yourselves just holding your BlackBerry of choice, and then, without even pressing down, just finding your thumbs always absently scrolling your trackball? Does you find the feeling of the rolling the trackball underneath your thumbs a strange comfort? Does you sometimes fidget with your BlackBerry, re-reading messages and texts that you read before for no apparent reason, but just to be interacting with the thing?

Is your BlackBerry first thing you look at in the morning, and the last thing you see before bed? Do you wake up in the middle of the night (maybe a dream woke you up, who knows?) and find that your first instinct is to look for a red blinking thing on your bedside table? Is any of this sounding familiar?

I sit at work on my computer, and I probably glance at my BlackBerry at least once every few minutes. Even if there are no messages blinking, I still press a button to see the screen come alive and to admire the menu...

I ponder sometimes what exactly it is about this thing that I so adore. I'd like to think that I functioned perfectly well before I purchased my first BlackBerry (this is my third). My friend asked me last week (she has no interest in BlackBerry smartphones or smartphones of any sort) what it is exactly that I love so much about my BlackBerry. I had a flood of reasons come to my mind, such as the cute form factor, the unbelievable reliability of the device, the push email, and so on. But in trying to pinpoint the most poignant reason, I kinda became quiet. I actually needed a moment to give her a really honest response.

I said to her: "You know, Laura, I think the reason why I love my BlackBerry so much is because, ever since I've gotten this thing, it's made it so much easier to keep in touch with all of the people that I care about the most." And that's the truth. At the end of the day, what does my BlackBerry do for me? It keeps me in perfect contact, whether through lightning-fast emails, texts (made more pleasurable by the Curve's awesome keyboard), Messenger, or through PIN #'s with the people most important to me—my family and friends.

So I guess when I say that I'm addicted to my BlackBerry, it's another way of saying that I'm addicted to my people! Ha ha ha!

Cheers everyone, and cherish your BlackBerry!

—incognito.girly, CrackBerry.com Member

All this being said—and most of it is true—we do need to bear in mind Step 2 on the path towards BlackBerry recovery: *Believe in things more important than our BlackBerry.*

We may find it hard to grasp what, or more importantly, *who*, is more important than our BlackBerry. We will come to understand this better as we progress through the steps outlined in this book.

"Step Away from the BlackBerry"

In this chapter, we will walk you through Step 3 of overcoming your BlackBerry addiction: learning to occasionally live *without* your BlackBerry.

Step 3:
Begin to Turn Away
from BlackBerry Abuse

Step 3: Begin to turn away from BlackBerry abuse. We resolve to begin occasionally turning our will and our lives over to the power of being BlackBerryless.

> *In other words, the third step in overcoming our addiction is to begin to take short breaks from our BlackBerry.*

Along our path away from the abuse of our BlackBerry smartphones, we come to our third chapter in this book. The third step in the traditional path of recovery is to turn our lives and our will over to a higher power. We suggest that Step 3 towards BlackBerry recovery is to step away from our BlackBerry for a bit. Doing so lets us free ourselves from the shackles that enslave us and remember what it is that gives meaning to our lives.

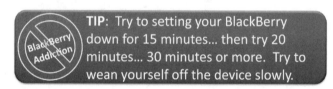

TIP: Try to setting your BlackBerry down for 15 minutes... then try 20 minutes... 30 minutes or more. Try to wean yourself off the device slowly.

■ **Caution** Exercising while checking Email is not Relaxing.

Recent studies have shown that the constant interruption of reading and replying to email or otherwise multitasking while you exercise can be more fatiguing than relaxing. According to Mark Berman, a University of Michigan neuroscientist, "People think they're refreshing themselves [by exercise], but they're fatiguing themselves."[1]

For some, this might mean connecting with our higher power. For others, it might mean re-connecting with our spouse or partner. And for others, it might just mean enjoying time with our kids or enjoying the great outdoors. There is life beyond our BlackBerry; we just have to let ourselves find it.

---

[1] Source: Digital Devices Deprive Brain of Needed Downtime by Matt Richtel, Aug 24, 2010, New York Times.

" Cannot Turn It Off

I turned my BlackBerry off for hours at a time only to turn it back on and find text and email messages. I now keep it on vibrate even at the movies.

—Lenny M.

Almost every 6 months, I say that's it. To save my sanity and my marriage, I will put it away. I stop the data portion and use it as a phone and agenda only. That lasts for exactly two days!

—Jonathan D.

I've even turned my BlackBerry off only to find myself kinda accidently turning it back on and then just leaving it on.

—Oscar M.

I have sleeping problems, and I often find myself picking up my BlackBerry throughout the night. Then, I tell myself I need to put it down and try to sleep.

—Moe

"

83% of People Check Email while on Vacation!

Source: AOL Email Addiction Survey

Gary's wife Gloria recently challenged him to go out of town with her and leave his BlackBerry behind. She didn't think he could do this. And, at the time of updating this second edition of the CrackBerry book, two years later, he has yet to do it. However, she really pushed him to just go away with her and not take the added stress and work with him.

Of course, Gary balked at the mere mention of this idea:

Said Gary: "I have to take my BlackBerry; what if my kids need me? Or, what if one of my students has to get in touch with me? Or my business parter needs me to follow up on something?"

The excuses he gave illustrate the main reasons why we are so reluctant to step away from our BlackBerry smartphones for an extended period of time:

- We are afraid to leave it behind: Our fear comes in many shapes and sizes, but it can be paralyzing. We are afraid to journey too far without our BlackBerry.

- We fear we may learn we aren't really indispensible: Much of our self-worth is tied into the things we do, and it's comforting to think we are so important that others can't live without us. It would be sobering to learn others don't really need us.

- We fear we won't know what to do if we don't have our BlackBerry to check email, news updates, weather, and the like: We are creatures of habit, and breaking that mold is not easy.

Fear keeps us from doing many things in our lives. Sometimes, healthy fear actually drives us to pursue our dreams and hopes, but sometimes fear can be paralyzing. We have all heard the famous cliché: "There is nothing to fear, but fear itself." Yet, everyone has fears. The question at hand for us is:

What is it that the BlackBerry user fears about being away from his or her BlackBerry?

One answer is something we touched on in Chapter 1. We like to be in touch, and we like to feel needed. When that little red light goes off or the holster vibrates, we know that someone is looking for us, and that can be affirming (or comforting). We have a fear of not being wanted or needed.

Most of us have a very basic desire to be needed by others. Having our loved ones depend on us is not a burden, so much as it is something that provides meaning to the very fabric of our existence.

"The entire sum of existence is the magic of being needed by just one person."

—V.I. Putnam

When we are connected through our BlackBerry smartphones, we feel needed and thus, fulfilled. If we leave our BlackBerry behind, then it's possible we'll discover that the world really can go on without us being in constant contact.

This leads us to the second reason we are reluctant to leave our BlackBerry smartphones behind: maybe we really aren't indispensible after all. This certainly builds upon what we just stated before; life can (and will) go on without us. The important thing for us to realize is that *we* can go on without the day-to-day hustle-and-bustle of BlackBerry-tethered life, too—for a little while, anyway.

Nobody is indispensible. Even the President has a Vice President—just in case. Our co-workers, friends, and business associates will survive if we are out of touch for a *few hours* or even a *few days*. Essentially, this, too, relates to fear. We are afraid that we can be replaced, forgotten, or just not needed.

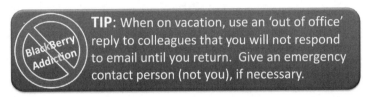

TIP: When on vacation, use an 'out of office' reply to colleagues that you will not respond to email until you return. Give an emergency contact person (not you), if necessary.

So, the answer is that we just have to get over ourselves. We are not that important or indispensible—no one is. Life will wait for us to return; it won't bypass us just because our BlackBerry is at home. Keep this in mind!

Finally, we are creatures of habit, and we don't like change. Few people do. Now, some people are more adventurous than others, but the third reason for our reluctance to step away from the BlackBerry and see the higher powers in our world is that we don't know what to do when we aren't on the device.

❝ BlackBerry in Shower

I'm guilty of using my BlackBerry just about everywhere. But my main confession is 'Berrying in the shower. I actually keep a Ziploc bag in the bathroom, just so I can do this. I know: I'm pathetic. And you know what: I don't care. LOL! I'm addicted and not looking for a cure!

— johnj41, Pinstack.com forums moderator ❞

Change is all about fear (funny how this all connects, isn't it?). We are afraid to find out what we must do if our BlackBerry is not with us. So, here is the task for all BlackBerry abusers: take the plunge, conquer the fear, and just put it down, if only for a little bit. Go ahead: try 15 minutes first, then move on to 30 minutes, and even longer time periods. You may feel liberated and free.

The World Stops Without My BlackBerry

I know I am a CrackBerry addict because, when I see someone else with a BlackBerry, I smile at them. I do this because I know they have the same addiction. Every morning when I wake up, the first thing I reach for under my pillow is my BlackBerry. I check how many emails I have in the four hours since I put it down to sleep.

After I finish getting ready for work, I am walking to the bus stop, checking the news for the morning on my 'Berry. Once I get on the bus, I watch one or two videos from YouTube that I downloaded the previous night. Then, after I get off the bus to transfer to the train, I start jammin' to my music while responding to my emails. When I reach the office, I send a BlackBerry message to my wife that I've arrived at work safely without crashing into a door. [Editor's Note: A BlackBerry message is sent from the BlackBerry Messenger *instant messaging (IM) application.]*

Upon arriving to work, I buy a cup of coffee, and I check www.digg.com *for the latest news. By midday, I am sharing jokes with friends through email or Google chat and surfing* www.CrackBerry.com*'s blogs and forums for the latest news about BlackBerry.*

When it's time to leave work, I give my 'Berry a little charge to make sure it's full, in case there's a train delay. While on the train home, I make sure that I check Viigo for the latest news through its RSS feed, and I tag the ones that I want to read before I go to bed [Editor's Note: Viigo is an RSS (Really Simple Syndication) Newsreader for the BlackBerry].

Right before I go to bed, I blog on my BlackBerry and send it out as a general email. Finally, I slip it under my pillow, so I can feel it vibrate if someone responds to me.

I am a BlackBerry Addict.

I must have it with me or the world stops.

—Dwayne, CrackBerry.com Member

Of course, some of us find it frightening to be without our BlackBerry, even for a short while (see the story, "Fear of Losing My BlackBerry").

Fear of Losing My BlackBerry

I must start by setting the stage of this story. We all know how the winters up here in Canada are; let's just say white. During early spring, we have the inevitable melt, where everything gets excessively wet and puddly. It was at this time of year when a simple and normal act turned into a tragic and terrible night.

I am, as most BlackBerry users will understand, a quick-draw user. I never have my BlackBerry much farther than an arm's length away. My BlackBerry sits on my right hip, in various holsters and pouches.

So one night I was heading out to grab a bite to eat. I nonchalantly walked out to my car, opened the door, and stepped over the large puddle that I parked on. And there it went: crack, splash! My beloved 'Berry was in the water, face down. I picked it up as quickly as I could, sacrificing the dryness of my foot and knee as I instinctively knelt down in the middle of the puddle. I pulled it out of the holster. And, as if to taunt me, the screen flickered, showed the hour glass, and went black. I quickly pulled the battery out and took it inside. Pacing around my kitchen, I pondered what my next step would be to save it. I had a bottle of distilled water for use in various automotive applications, so I doused it in the water to rinse off any road salt, and then I stuck it under a hair dryer on low for a few minutes.

A couple of days later, I decided to risk the first power on since the swim. To my surprise, it turned on and booted up to the Home screen. I went to run through the menu, but every single key failed to work, and the trackwheel did nothing. I was devastated. I felt like I had just broken up with a girlfriend; more shockingly, I felt like I'd been dumped. I would search for it, long for it.

My days were spent trying to figure out how to text message without a full keyboard (QWERTY) keypad. I was chained to my desk, and every email was a chore to read. I was going through serious withdrawal. I went for about three days before I couldn't take using a boring old cell phone, and I went out and got a new BlackBerry. I love it. And it has been a match made in heaven ever since.

To anyone who has lost his BlackBerry to a tragedy such as this, there is a light at the end of the tunnel.

—Kieran, CrackBerry.com Member

As sad as some of these stories are, perhaps what is sadder is that many readers of this book can truly relate. We are attached to our beloved BlackBerry smartphones. We don't want to be away from them, even for a minute.

Here is something to think about: Most of us long-time BlackBerry owners may have experienced a *memory leak* on our older devices. When this happens, the hour glass just turns and turns, and the BlackBerry has 0 bytes of free memory. The solution to this problem is to give the BlackBerry a break and do a *battery pull*, where you just open the back, take out the battery, let the device rest, and then put the battery back in. When the 'Berry powers up, its memory is restored.

Maybe the same can be said for us. Maybe when we use the BlackBerry too much, we get our own memory leak and forget about those more important things in life. So, take some time, step away from the BlackBerry, and let your mind reboot from time to time, as well!

"BlackBerry Boo-Boos"

In this chapter, we will walk you through Step 4 of overcoming your BlackBerry addiction: facing your faux pas and resolving to do better. We will guide you through a "moral inventory" of BlackBerry use and abuse. And also, we will look at how your BlackBerry abuse has hurt those around you so we can begin to walk a path towards responsible BlackBerry use.

Step 4:
Take a Moral Inventory of Our BlackBerry Abuses

Step 4: Take a moral inventory of our BlackBerry abuses. We create a general list of those times we behaved poorly or even in a way that was dangerous to those around us.

In other words, the fourth step requires that we take a moral inventory *of those times when our BlackBerry use caused harm to those around us.*

Congratulations! You are making progress. You didn't throw this book away or put it up for sale on Ebay (not yet, anyway!) By now, you know you might have a problem. You are a BlackBerry overuser and maybe even a BlackBerry abuser. Don't fret; we are walking you through a process here. This process will help you restore some meaning to your life and allow you to live untethered from your BlackBerry, at least for short stretches at a time.

Along the path of recovery, the fourth phase or step is to search your soul and take a moral inventory. We'll wait while you do this... OK, you are in trouble, aren't you? Taking a moral inventory of our BlackBerry use means that we have to reflect on the times we were rude, thoughtless, unkind, selfish, and reckless for the sake of our BlackBerry use.

The BlackBerry Alphabetic Acrostic

On the Jewish holy day of Yom Kippur (AKA, the Day of Atonement), Jews recite an alphabetical acrostic of sins they have committed during the year. Performing this recitation sort of *frees* and *cleanses* them. We wonder what our BlackBerry alphabetical acrostic of sins might look like. We were all of the following:

- Arrogant in our email use.
- Boasted about our new BlackBerry.
- Caustic in our messaging.
- Diabolical in checking email under the table.
- Exclusive in only being nice to other BlackBerry users.

- Fraudulent when we said, "Honey, no, I wasn't checking email."
- Giddy when the new 'Berry showed up.
- Haughty when we upgraded to BlackBerry 6.0 and our friends were stuck on 5.0.
- Idolatrous in our worshiping our BlackBerry.
- Jealous when the guy on the train had a signal, and we didn't.
- Kissed our BlackBerry when we thought we had lost it.
- Lusted after the newest models.
- Malicious when we had to call tech support.
- Narrow Minded in our views of Android and iPhone users.
- Obstinate in our defending the BlackBerry at all costs.
- Punitive when we found someone who still was on a Palm.
- Querulous while talking on the BlackBerry.
- Removed from family life due to BlackBerry overuse.
- Stealthy and Sneaky in checking email.
- Treacherous to others in our car and on the road.
- Used other people's Wi-Fi—because we could.
- Violated basic rules of etiquette more than once with our devices.
- Worried more about our email going through than other, more important things.
- Xenophobic of those using a different operating system on their handheld.
- Yelled at our kids because they dropped our beloved BlackBerry.
- Zealous with our BlackBerry-related spending this past year.

Our BlackBerry boo-boos are an alphabet of woe!

We have all done something rude or inappropriate with our BlackBerry at some point. It can be as innocuous as not turning the profile to vibrate at the movies or as rude as texting during services at a wedding or a funeral. The list of possibilities is endless, and you will read some stories from the worst offenders later in this chapter.

66 BlackBerry Football Instead of Dancing with the Wife

One Saturday evening a few weeks ago, my wife and I were guests at a wedding reception. We sat at the same table with our very close friends, Larry and Dara. Larry and I are avid football fans of a particular college. That college was playing a football game the same night as the wedding reception, so we couldn't watch or attend the game.

The next best option was to get updates of the game during the reception on my friend's BlackBerry. So, for most of the party, Larry and I passed his BlackBerry back and forth to get play-by-play updates, when we should have been enjoying our wives' company, dancing, and being sociable.

We would even interrupt the conversation to tell each other when big plays occurred. When I arrived home after the reception, I found out very quickly from my wife that she was very unhappy about my evening's addiction to the college football game updates on the BlackBerry.

The next morning at church, I shared with Larry how I got in trouble for watching the BlackBerry at the reception. Larry said, "I got in trouble too!"

—Ed P., an Accountant in Florida 99

The question we have to ask ourselves is this: "Why are we rude with our BlackBerry smartphones?"

We all know basic etiquette. We know what we won't tolerate in others, so why do we tolerate and justify these actions when we do them? Maybe we are just addicted to college football, and the BlackBerry is just a means to an end.

A psychologist might tell us that this is a classic sign of addiction: justiying behavior in ourselves that we would not tolerate from others. Our parents would just say we were being selfish and rude. It could be both.

There are a few possible reasons as to why so many of us commit BlackBerry boo-boos:

- We truly can't help ourselves (this is why we need this book).

- We aren't even aware of what we are doing because we are so focused on the BlackBerry.

- We somehow think that rules of common decency and etiquette don't apply to us.

- We believe that the BlackBerry is so unique and special that there no rules that should apply when we use it.

If we can't help ourselves, then we do need some sort of help to gain control over our BlackBerry use. We need to ask ourselves if this kind of behavior is in response to our BlackBerry usage, or if it extends to other areas of our lives. Once we make this determination, we can begin to formulate a plan to address our behavior.

If you are someone who feels that the laws of common decency don't apply to you, please do the following:

1. Place your BlackBerry in your freezer for about an hour.

2. Remove it from the freezer.

3. Place your BlackBerry between your thumb and forefinger.

4. Finally, please hit yourself in the head with your now frozen BlackBerry as hard as you can—you deserve it!

There is nothing—repeat nothing—that makes you superior because you have the latest and coolest smartphone on the market. As cool as the BlackBerry is, you still have to function on planet earth with all the rules of etiquette and decency that apply to everyone else.

If you believe that "the BlackBerry is so unique and special that no rules should apply"— well, you may be correct, but please re-read the freezer suggestion just oulined. One thing is certain: There are others in this world who are worse than you when it comes to BlackBerry abuse. Just read on to see how bad things could get if you don't attempt to change your behavior!

❝ Embarrassing Ringtone!

For fun, I downloaded and installed an alert on my BlackBerry Pearl that plays the sound of a woman in ecstasy at the peak of sexual response. The alert would activate, "Oooooooooh! Ahhhh! Ohhh! Oh Yes! YES! YES!" each time I received a text message or an email. It was controversial and fun, and I enjoyed the attention my alert tone received from my friends.

There's a time and a place for everything, however. Professionally, I teach psychology at a small, private college. During class, I religiously turn off my BlackBerry; or at least, I reduce the sound and revert to vibration mode. But I forgot to do this on a particularly important day.

It was the first class of Winter semester, and every seat in the classroom was taken by new students. Part of my lecture and introduction to new students is to review the rules of cell phone usage. This helps to manage the noise level and reduce the number of interruptions. The first rule, of course, is that cell phones should be turned to either the off or vibrate position.

I had just made my points to all and was feeling pretty proud that I had their full attention and compliance. That didn't last very long. Within moments, the sound of sex emitted from my BlackBerry in its hip holster. The setting was on Loud and all in the room heard it: "Oooooooh! Ahhhh! Ohhh! Oh Yes! YES! YES!"

I fumbled for the phone to turn it off and explained to the class, "This is a demonstration of what not to do in my class!"

—Doreen, Psychology Professor 🙶

So far we have made a moral inventory of our BlackBerry use and abuse. All of us probably find ourselves lacking in some way. Maybe we are even saddened and embarrassed by the reality of our rude and selfish behavior. Keep reading. In the rest of this chapter, we'll cover strategies that will help you restore order to your life and curb your bad BlackBerry behavior.

🙶 *See my addiction, my attachment to....my BlackBerry.*
I'm posting this while sitting, waiting in a sushi bar downtown...
I came out here to have a few sushi rolls for lunch with my girlfriend.
When we finished eating and received the check, I found that my pockets were empty. None of the usual items I carry were on my person. No chapstick, no change, no credit cards, no I.D., NO MONEY! I left them all at home! I remember setting those things aside before taking a shower to go out to eat. So, I sent my girlfriend home to get my money to pay for the meal. Meanwhile, I'm sitting here in the restaurant with the one thing I didn't forget - "I never leave home without it." Can you guess what that is?
My BlackBerry.

—Rive50What, CrackBerry.com Member 🙶

Taking a Moral Inventory of BlackBerry Abuses

Now it's time for a simple exercise. Simply list those times you have abused others with the incorrect, rude, or otherwise improper use of your BlackBerry. (And don't be shy; feel free to add more lines below if you need them!)

1. _____

_____

_____

_____

_____

_____

_____

_____

_____

_____

_____

"Am I a BlackBerry Abuser?"

In this chapter, we will walk you through Step 5 of overcoming your BlackBerry addiction: analyzing the user quiz we will take in this chapter and admitting to our specific BlackBerry abuses.

Step 5:
Admit to Our Specific BlackBerry Abuses

Step 5: Admit to our specific BlackBerry abuses. We will take the Addiction quiz and confess to our specific list of BlackBerry abuses. Then , we will share this confession with the universe, ourselves, and another human.

In other words, we use Step 5 to admit to ourselves and others that we have been, and are, BlackBerry abusers.

Up until this point in the book, we have examined our behavior and shared stories that maybe made us laugh. Some of the stories and anecdotes might have struck a chord, while others might have struck a little too close to home. Chances are, you would not be reading this book unless, in some way, you or someone you love thought you might in fact be a BlackBerry over-user or abuser.

While there is no hard and fast empirical method to determine who is a BlackBerry abuser, there are some ways that we can begin to diagnose our behavior and help us learn whether we are in the at-risk group for BlackBerry abuse.

> ## "I have one friend who does not have a 'Berry. I offered to buy him one just so it would make my life easier if he had one."
>
> Source: Chad, CrackBerry.com Member

Certainly, one determining factor is the perception of others. How many times in a day does someone say to you, "Are you on that thing again?" Or, "Can you go five minutes without checking that?"

Do you take your BlackBerry to bed? When you wake up in the morning, do you first kiss your spouse first—or check your email? How long can you go without seeing whether you have new email?

Our guess is that your answers to the questions just asked will give you some indication as to whether you are in the at-risk group for being considered a BlackBerry abuser.

One of our goals with this book is to collect some empirical data or at least give users some true objective criteria for determining whether they are in need of BlackBerry rehab. On the following pages, you'll find a BlackBerry Use and Abuse quiz. We would like you to take this quiz to help determine your BlackBerry abuse status. Remember, honest answers are needed; you aren't showing this to anyone but yourself, right? So, what would it say about you if you lied on a test that was only meant for your own personal edification?

The BlackBerry Addiction Quiz

What follows is the BlackBerry Addiction quiz. Taking this quiz can help you determine whether you might be in the at-risk group for being a BlackBerry abuser. Please consider the questions carefully and answer truthfully, **Yes** or **No**.

No.	Question	My Answer	
1	Have you ever wanted to stop using your BlackBerry and found that you just couldn't?	Yes	No
2	Do you think about using your BlackBerry constantly?	Yes	No
3	Do you constantly check your BlackBerry, even when you know there is no new email?	Yes	No
4	Do you ever sneak away from people or groups to use your BlackBerry, without anyone else knowing?	Yes	No
5	Do you deny it when asked if you were just using your BlackBerry?	Yes	No
6	Do you have to check your BlackBerry before bed and immediately upon waking?	Yes	No
7	Do you use your BlackBerry in the bathroom?	Yes	No
8	Do you wish you could use your BlackBerry in the shower, too?	Yes	No
9	Have you ever ignored others in a conversation to use your BlackBerry?	Yes	No
10	Have you ever checked your BlackBerry while at a meal with others?	Yes	No
11	Have you ever checked your BlackBerry while at a stop light?	Yes	No
12	Have you ever read your BlackBerry while driving your vehicle?	Yes	No
13	Have you ever typed on your BlackBerry while driving a vehicle?	Yes	No
14	Do you check your BlackBerry while riding your bike or walking on a busy street?	Yes	No

No.	Question	My Answer	
15	Have you ever bumped into someone because you were paying attention to your BlackBerry instead of paying attention to your surroundings?	Yes	No
16	Have you ever put down your BlackBerry, swearing that you will not use it, and then find yourself picking it up again shortly afterward?	Yes	No
17	Do you try to stop using your BlackBerry on weekends and on vacation, but just can't?	Yes	No
18	Do you feel that you have to check your BlackBerry **at least** once every hour outside work hours?	Yes	No
19	Do you feel that you have to check your BlackBerry **at least** once every 30 minutes during the work day?	Yes	No
20	Do you use your BlackBerry even when you know there are no emails or calls that have to be answered before the next work day?	Yes	No
21	Has anyone ever approached you with concern about your BlackBerry use?	Yes	No
22	Do you have multiple backup batteries or multiple charging cables, so you can be sure that your BlackBerry is never without power?	Yes	No
23	Do you have a backup BlackBerry handheld, in case your current one breaks or fails?	Yes	No
24	Do you spend more than 30 minutes a day doing anything on your BlackBerry?	Yes	No
25	Do you play games on your BlackBerry (for more than 30 minutes/week)?	Yes	No
26	Do you feel "lost" or "naked" when you don't have your BlackBerry with you?	Yes	No
27	Do you feel hopeless about your relationship with your BlackBerry?	Yes	No

Next, tally up your **Yes** answers: (*Be honest!*) _____

Also, ask yourself this: Are there other abuses that were not listed in the quiz that you should admit to?

Assessing Your Addiction Quiz Results

Now check out the following chart to find out where you stand on the BlackBerry Addiction scale.

# of Yes Answers	What this Means
0	No Addiction (Are you being honest?)
1-5	Mild Addiction
6-10	Medium Addiction
11-15	Strong Addiction
16-20	Painful Addiction
20+	Beyond Addiction and into Obsession (Get help now!)

helpful to you. One thing to be aware of is that BlackBerry addiction is a slippery slope; you may say **Yes** to only a few questions today, but it's quite possible that the number will grow substantially in a few weeks. The longer you use your device, the more likely your list is to grow.

" I had 11 "yes" responses, making me "Strongly Addicted".
I knew I was addicted long before this quiz came out, though. I was once in the bathroom at work, thumb typing away on BBM with a close friend, when I heard the door open and someone enter the stall next to me. To my utter chagrin, it was one of my coworkers that knows me well. The conversation went like this:
Coworker: Oh my God, Tina, is that you? Me: Uh, yes. Hi. Coworker: Are you typing on your Blackberry? Me (now breaking out into an embarrassed sweat): Uh, yes. I was. Coworker: I come in here to do that all the time too! Both of us just laughed at that point.
Needless to say, I am not the only Blackberry addict in my office, though I've got it bad!

—Teenerfed, CrackBerry Member "

❝ Sneaking Away from Groups

I usually sneak away, but it usually involves an excuse such as, "I have to use the restroom."

—Helen Ann R.

After I return from sneaking off, I see everyone smiling when I return to the group holding my BlackBerry.

—Lenny M.

Sometimes when I'm on vacation, I try to distance myself from my lady friend, so she does not know I checked in at my office while on vacation. I don't always want her to know my mind is at work again.

—Duane S.

Sometimes I sneak away. Usually I don't mind using it in front of other people, but when dining (people close to me get easily irritated at the amount of attention it gets), I will place it on my lap and use it under the tabletop.

—Moe ❞

Could we be in denial about our BlackBerry Abuses?

❝ Cash Penalties for Use in a Meeting

My Sales Manager has implemented a new rule: if she catches us on our BlackBerry smartphones during a Sales meeting, we have to pay $10 per occurrence! Needless to say, we have quite a bit of money in our BlackBerry fund. We have not decided what these funds will be used for, but at the rate it is going, we will be able to throw an end-of-the-year celebration!

—Agustin "Agie" O. ❞

❝ Kevin's Comments on the Addiction Quiz

*When I took this quiz, I basically said **Yes** to everything except question 27: I didn't feel hopeless about my BlackBerry use because I felt it was something I had control over. To some extent, I do have that control. However, one thing I have noticed from working on this book is that I now suffer from a self-induced case of ADD (attention deficit disorder), and I think my BlackBerry is to blame. There was a time when I liked nothing better than to sit down and focus on a long task from start to finish because I found it a rewarding experience. Now, thanks to the BlackBerry, I live my life a few minutes at a time—the time between checking messages and new notifications on my BlackBerry. I've become extremely efficient at getting little things done quickly, but it's become impossible for me to do anything effectively that takes longer than a few minutes. Just ask Gary and Martin how difficult it's been to write this book with me!* ❞

❝ Martin's Comments on the Quiz

Unlike Kevin, I only answered "Yes" to 24 of the 27 questions – I'm way ahead! But, I thought it might be helpful to share a few additional details:

- **Question 8. Do you wish you could use it in the shower?** *I answered No because my showers only last about 3 minutes (my hair is really short). If my showers were longer, I might be breaking out the Ziploc bag for BlackBerry shower use. (Kevin told me he sometimes takes baths so he can use his BlackBerry.)*
- **Question 15. Ever bump into anyone?** *I answered No because I believe I am an adept multitasker. I only take glances at the BlackBerry when I'm sure no one is anywhere near me. Also, here in Ormond Beach, Florida, I rarely walk where there are lots of other people. Most of the time, the only things I would bump into are my dogs, Belle, Pixie and Wolfie—and they know how to keep their distance.*
- **Question 23. Do you have backup BlackBerry smartphones?** *Being in the BlackBerry video and training business, I actually have three to five working BlackBerry smartphones at any one time.*

- Question 25. Do you play games on your BlackBerry? *I'm too busy doing other things on my BlackBerry to play games.*
- Question 27. Do you feel helpless with your BlackBerry? *No. I feel I'm in total control of this device. At least, that's what I keep telling myself!*

" Musings of a BlackBerry Abuser

I take pride in the level of my intelligence. I like to think that I know a little more than the average person. Once, during a game of Cranium, I got the answer wrong on a particular question, but I felt my answer was correct. I pulled out my 'Berry and Googled it. As it turned out, after about 20 minutes of research, I was, in fact, incorrect. Now anytime a matter is in question, my friends always challenge me to Google it with my 'Berry. For the record, I'm usually right!

During Church, my friend and I make commentary on the sermon using the BlackBerry Messenger *program, even though we may be sitting right next to each other.*

I return e-mails while on the toilet.

When I'm downstairs and my wife is upstairs, I talk to her with the BlackBerry Messenger *program, so I won't have to get out of my recliner.*

I have one friend who does not have a 'Berry. I offered to buy him one, just so it would make my life easier if he had one.

Once, while being intimate with my wife, my 'Berry was on the night stand, and I received an e-mail. I wasn't going to check it, but my wife could tell that it was killing me to know who emailed me. She made me check it so I could get back to focusing on the matter at hand.

—Chad, a www.CrackBerry.com *member* "

66 Dual Addiction

Not long ago, my wife joined forces with me and finally got a BlackBerry. Well, Friday night she was in the hospital doubled over in severe pain. They kept running test after test. While I was waiting, I got online to several sites and got a great idea.

Why not surf with two BlackBerry smartphones at once?

My wife handed hers over to me, and it was great. While one was loading pages, I could play the BrickBreaker game with the other. I could also surf and type emails. I now think two BlackBerry smartphones is the way to go.

By the way, I cleared it with the nurse before I was surfing away. And my wife is fine, but she wanted her BlackBerry back.

—Johnny D, CrackBerry.com Member 99

One measure of our addiction are the hoops we jump through just to get these devices in the first place!

Can you relate to these stories? Are you thinking that this book really was written with you in mind? Did you score more than 10 on the quiz? Chances are that the person who bought you this book thinks you should have scored even higher!

The first step is for you to admit your problem, especially since you can now see it in black and white. You need to keep reading, take copious notes, and resolve to make some important changes in your BlackBerry use. Good luck to you!

"OK, I Am a BlackBerry Abuser"

In this chapter, we will walk you through Step 6 of overcoming your BlackBerry addiction: becoming more responsible in how you use your BlackBerry.

There is a time and a place to use your BlackBerry – and it isn't **all** the time and everyplace – no matter what your BlackBerry Addiction Quiz says!

> ### Step 6:
> #### Plan to Be a More
> #### Responsible BlackBerry User

Step 6: Plan to be a more responsible BlackBerry user. We commit to begin addressing our shortcomings and BlackBerry-related character defects.

In other words, Step 6 is where you freely admit you are a BlackBerry abuser and start to fix some of your errant ways.

Still reading the book, huh? Our guess is that means you didn't do so well on the quiz in the last chapter. Don't worry. As many in the field of addiction say: "The first step to recovery is admitting the problem." So, you have a problem. You can't put your BlackBerry down. You use your BlackBerry too much. You bring your BlackBerry into the bathroom, the bedroom, the dining room, and everywhere else.

We can help you, but first you have to resolve to make some significant changes in your behavior. If you are willing to see that you are, in fact, a CrackBerry Addict, then you're ready to move forward. We'll wait for you... OK, we agree. You're a CrackBerry Addict, so let's move on.

A study by Rutgers University Professor Gayle Porter blames BlackBerry for fueling a spike in email and Internet addiction. The key symptom: You can only go a few minutes without checking for new email.

The good professor goes on to say that these addictive effects can be devastating, and that employers should really realize that "addiction to technology" can be equally as "damaging to a worker's mental health" as chemical or substance addictions. One key sign of a user being addicted is if she focuses on her BlackBerry while ignoring those around her.

> **<u>Key Addiction Sign</u>:**
> **Ignore those around you in order to focus on your BlackBerry.**

The Work-Life Balance

You need to begin thinking honestly about your BlackBerry use in both your personal and professional life. Imagine there were a balance scale that showed the balance of your work and personal lives. If so, would such a scale show a reasonable balance between these lives, or would your BlackBerry use weight the scale significantly toward the work side)?

BlackBerry: A Help or Hindrance to your Balance?

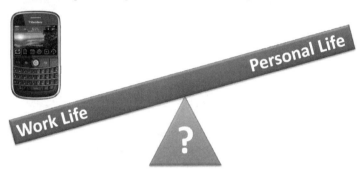

The key to recovery from any addiction is *self-realization*. You need to admit to yourself that you do indeed have a problem. Only after you admit to the addiction problem can you realistically begin charting a path to a more balanced life.

Seeing the Light at the End of the Tunnel

Unlike most of the things tied to the word *addiction* (e.g., drugs, gambling, and alcohol), the BlackBerry is, by design, a useful tool that can increase your productivity, save you time, and even allow you to balance your work and personal lives better.

TIP: Set your 'personal' appointments (spouse, kids, friends) on your BlackBerry with equal priority to your Work appointments... and keep them!

There are countless examples of people saving an hour a day because they are now converting what was once downtime into productive time.

For example, Gary shares: "I have increased my personal productivity and balance by using my BlackBerry. How? I put personal and work appointments in my BlackBerry. I set limits on when I use it. I realize when I'm doing something negative, and I try to stop these negative actions from becoming a habit.

Sure, I'm slightly addicted, but I realize it, and I work to control it. With any addiction, it takes constant vigilance to keep it in check. Unlike most addictions, you can use the BlackBerry to improve your life and the lives of those around you—in both work and personal arenas!"

Let's take a step back from the personal side of BlackBerry addiction and look at some anecdotal numbers for the problem.

Lakefront Cookout

Our lake club has an end of the season cookout that is for adults only. We set up tables on the beach and out onto the main dock, light up the tiki torches, and serve up the BBQ and drinks; the emphasis here is on drinks.

I'm at the end table on the outermost portion of the main dock, and I'm sitting at the very end of this table. The night progresses wonderfully, with good friends sharing a meal and some fun conversation.

After participating in the discussions, jokes, and general banter, I became a bit quiet. My wife noticed, but she was having too good a time to really pay attention. She and her girlfriends were laughing up a storm and putting the red wine away at a blistering pace, so my sudden change in demeanor was a very minor concern to her.

What she didn't know was that I was using the BlackBerry Messenger program and carrying on two simultaneous conversations. I had my BlackBerry down in my lap, just under the edge of the table, and I was texting away like mad. There must have been a lull in the conversation at the table just as I received a joke from my BlackBerry buddy in L.A. (I'm in Northern New Jersey).

I let out a loud snort and started to laugh pretty hard, and it drew the attention of everyone around me at the table. Suddenly my wife realized what I was doing and shot me a frigid look. I was on vacation from work, at the last party of the year at the lake, and I darn well ought to be paying attention to my friends. Rather than yell at me from five seats away, she whipped out her own cell phone and sent me a one word text message: "Stop!"

—Rambo47, BlackBerryForums.com Member

Addiction by the Numbers

Before the statistics professors roll their eyes and the professional pollsters toss their arms in the air, let me be honest and say that the numbers quoted here are not in any way scientifically rigorous. But, by the same measure, they do give us some sense of the numbers concerning BlackBerry addiction.

Recently, www.CrackBerry.com proudly announced that it had topped two and a half million members. Imagine that! More than two and a half million people have taken the time to register at a website called www.CrackBerry.com.

The Sheraton Hotel Study

A larger survey was conducted by Sheraton Hotels[1]. *In its survey of 6,500 traveling executives, 35 percent of the respondents said they would choose their smartphone over their spouse.* Of those polled, 87 percent said they bring their devices into the bedroom.

In the same survey, 84 percent of respondents said they check their emails just before they go to sleep. And another 80 percent said they check them in the morning, as soon as they get up.

Of those polled, 62 percent said they love their BlackBerry or PDA, and most of them said the device makes their life more productive.

---

[1] Source: September 15, 2008 survey from Sheraton Hotels, which is owned by Starwood Hotels and Resorts. You can view the survey results at this URL: www.starwoodhotels.com/sheraton/about/news/news_release_detail.html?obj_id=0900c7b9809c404f

> **Tip** As we strongly suggest throughout this book, you may want to direct more of your love to your spouse or family than your BlackBerry!

The survey also found that *more than three quarters of those polled say their gadgets give them more quality time with friends and family... and help them enjoy life more* [Author's note: Is this denial or what?].

> **Note** Here's something to keep in mind about the skewed sample populations. The www.CrackBerry.com survey is of people who have been motivated enough join a forum and ask technical questions about the BlackBerry. So it's quite likely that the sample of BlackBerry users is skewed toward those who are heavy users and may exhibit more addictive behavior than the general BlackBerry user population.

So, we need help. We use our BlackBerry smartphones too much. We've got a monkey on our back, and it comes from a Canadian company called RIM. We (or someone close to us) bought this book, for crying out loud! So we have a problem. But don't worry or panic; you can overcome this addiction, and we will help you.

Keep reading!

"Ask Others for Help"

In this chapter, we will walk you through Step 7 of overcoming your BlackBerry addiction: asking others for help in behaving more responsibly with your BlackBerry.

Step 7:
Ask for Help in Achieving Responsible BlackBerry Use

Step 7: Ask for help in achieving responsible BlackBerry use. We realize that we need help from those around us to become more responsible BlackBerry users. This might mean having others put our BlackBerry in safe place until we can learn to use it without hurting ourselves or others.

In the traditional Step 7 of the recovery process, recovering addicts humbly ask a higher power" to remove their shortcomings. That is a very important piece of the process for moving forward and restoring a healthy balance in our lives. We need to be able to "step away from the BlackBerry" for at least some period of time if we are to achieve that balance. Remember, the goal is to master the BlackBerry, not be a slave to it.

Who is the Master? You or Your BlackBerry?

One difficulty in stepping away from the BlackBerry is that these devices are extraordinarily multi-functional. We use them for one thing, the email indicator blinks or vibrates, and then we are right back to our addiction.

Two of the authors, Gary and Martin, are avid cyclists. Gary has the bad habit of using his BlackBerry as his primary MP3 player (in addition to all the other things he uses it for). So, how does this get him in trouble?

Gary will leave his house (in nice weather) early in the morning and start his beautiful, scenic ride towards the ocean. He has about 600 songs loaded on his memory card, and he has the playlist set to *shuffle* his favorite tunes. This is the true story of one morning ride that turned sour and reminded Gary that using a dedicated MP3 player might be the better way to exercise.

He leaves the house at 7:00 for a nice 30-mile ride. Five miles in, he stops at the beach to take in the sun and the sights. He makes his first mistake: he takes out the BlackBerry and starts to multitask. He notices the red light blinking and thinks: "It is an email from Martin; this could be important." Well, it was important, so now he feels that he can't wait until later to respond.

He takes a minute, now cooling down, to type a response. He hits send (the music is still going), and he gets back on the bike. 10 minutes later, the music stops and he hears Martin's ring tone. "What's the harm," he thinks as he pulls out his BlackBerry and takes the call. He then tells Martin that he is on his bike and needs to pull over. They talk for a minute and then Gary gets back on the bike, but again he sees the red light blinking. Like the fool he sometimes is, Gary checks the email and thinks, "This message is from Kevin; this might be important, too." You get the idea. Gary stops three more times on his 30-mile ride to answer phone calls and check email. The stress starts to build as he realizes that he now knows he has work waiting for him back at the house. "Next time" he resolves, "I will leave the BlackBerry and take the iPod. Or, I will turn off my wireless signal while I ride, accepting no emails, text messages or phone calls."

■ **Caution** As we mentioned earlier in the book. Research has shown that staying connected to electronic devices that cause constant interruptions, such as your BlackBerry, while trying to exercise can leave you more mentally fatigued than refreshed.

This is just one of many examples when we should know better and leave the BlackBerry behind. If we can't leave it behind, can we at least learn to ignore the temptation of checking in?

Here is another exercise for you. Ask yourselves the following questions— again, try to answer them honestly!

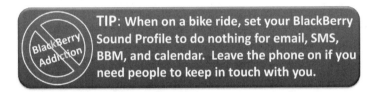

TIP: When on a bike ride, set your BlackBerry Sound Profile to do nothing for email, SMS, BBM, and calendar. Leave the phone on if you need people to keep in touch with you.

An Exercise: What Should You Do?

At first glance, these might seem similar to the BlackBerry Addiction quiz; however, these are meant to be ongoing scenario questions for you as you use your BlackBerry on a daily basis. We have tried to come up with a number of situations that could take you off track from being a responsible BlackBerry user. These questions will help you be more prepared to answer responsibly.

You are sitting in a meeting and your BlackBerry starts beeping. What should you do?

- *Addicted Choice*: Ignore others and check it out.

- *Better Choice*: Remember to turn your BlackBerry profile to **Silent** mode and don't look at it during the meeting.

You are riding in a limo with family members on the way to a funeral. What should you do?

- *Addicted Choice*: Ignore others and use your 'Berry.

- *Better Choice*: Remember to turn your BlackBerry profile to **Silent** mode and don't look at it during the ride.

Now it's time for you to write a few answers of your own.

You are sitting at a traffic light waiting for it to turn green. You have your child in the back of the car. What should you do?

- Addicted Choice:

- Better Choice:

You are driving down the road and your BlackBerry vibrates, telling you that new email has arrived. What should you do?

- Addicted Choice:

- Better Choice:

Your children are sitting around at home with your family in the evening, and you have an opportunity to check and use your BlackBerry. What should you do?

- Addicted Choice:

- Better Choice:

You're making dinner together with your spouse and your BlackBerry vibrates. What should you do?

You are walking down a busy city sidewalk, and your BlackBerry vibrates, saying email has arrived. What should you do?

You are sitting in the airport, surrounded by a bunch of strangers. Should you use your BlackBerry, or strike up a conversation?

You are walking into your work office and getting in the elevator. Should you be using your BlackBerry at this time?

You are on a field trip with your child's class, and one of the other parents is talking to you and your BlackBerry buzzes. What should you do?

You are talking with someone you just met at the local park, and your BlackBerry vibrates or beeps, saying you received a new message. What should you do?

You are at a meal with a colleague and your BlackBerry buzzes. What should you do?

You're talking with your colleagues at an informal meeting, and your BlackBerry buzzes. What should you do?

Do any of these situations sound familiar? If you can relate to these questions, then you probably use your BlackBerry too much. If you have any hesitation about what the right answer is, you need help.

Electronics Rehab Getaway

The BlackBerry phenomenon has not gone unnoticed in our world. Many joke about it, and some good capitalists have found ways to help those who can't seem to help themselves. In addition to buying copies of this book for all your BlackBerry using friends, think about a BlackBerry-free getaway.

Several hotels in the Canadian Rockies have now offered *Electronic Rehab Getaways*. When the guests check in, their BlackBerry smartphones and other electronic gadgets are locked up in the hotel safe for the duration of their stay. With this service, the hotel guests can unplug and enjoy their stay. Also, the rehab guests can benefit from meditation, herbal teas, and spas to help ease the pain of detachment from their trusty BlackBerry smartphone.

With recent prices ranging from CDN $499 to $529/night in the Fairmont Hotels in Jasper Park Lodge, Lake Louise, and Banff, this is significant investment to break your BlackBerry addiction[1]. You could also try reading and following the steps in this book; that might help you achieve a long-lasting result for a much lower investment!

Check out the Washington, DC CrackBerry Massage. See the writeup from Time.com on December 14, 2009.

---

[1] Source: The www.canada.com web site, from a 7/17/2008 article by Sarah McGinnis, Canwest News Service. You can learn more about this option at this URL: www.canada.com/vancouversun/news/story.html?id=63b6f3b0-be92-4ead-9b32-c9af20c3ef7d

CrackBerry Massage and Spa

Ideal for the high-strung professional, Washington's Lunar Massage Studio offers the Crackberry, a 20-min. hand, thumb and arm massage that targets the modern malady known as "digital thumb" — an overexerted appendage sore from constant BlackBerry and iPhone jabbing. Targeted kneading releases tension in key areas.

Owner Joanna Robinson says the treatment, created on a whim, is a perfect fit for the nation's capital: "I understand the D.C. nerdy culture and the young professional," she says, referring to the massive corps of 20- and 30-something associates and interns who storm Washington each year. The $26 hand massage is for "the people who work very hard but make very little."[2]

On a related note, various spas around the country are offering spa or massage treatments to help with the dreaded "BlackBerry Thumb" (sore thumb joints due to over-using your BlackBerry).

Massage for BlackBerry Thumb

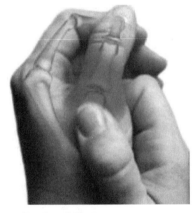

New York spa Graceful Services is joining a trend started by major U.S. hotels and is offering a "BlackBerry Finger Massage," according to My: Tech News. We don't know of anyone personally who has undergone such treatment, but we wouldn't be surprised to hear that it was frequented by a certain celebrity known to have a close personal attachment to her BlackBerry.[3]

Credit: CrackBerry.com

---

[2] Source Time Magazine:
http://www.time.com/time/specials/packages/article/0,28804,1947694_1947700_1947717,00.html#ixzz0wbika39C

[3] Source: http://news.cnet.com/8301-17938_105-9698603-1.html

We all need to step away from time to time. Too much of anything can be a bad thing, even too much BlackBerry. Like most things in our lives, when we step away—even for just a little while—we become much more appreciative of what we have when we step back into our regular world.

So, take a break. Go for a walk, or go out and appreciate nature or your family. And leave your BlackBerry at home. You will be OK. You can always get back to people later; they *will* wait for you.

"BlackBerry Bystanders"

In this chapter, we will walk you through Step 8 of overcoming your BlackBerry addiction: listing the innocent vicitims of your bad BlackBerry behavior.

> ## Step 8:
> ### List Those BlackBerry Bystanders We Have Wronged

Step 8: List those BlackBerry bystanders we have wronged. We will make a list of all those people (named and unnamed) that we have hurt because of our BlackBerry addiction.

In other words, Step 8 requires that we begin our attempt to redress those we have harmed. To do that, we need to identify who those people are.

Let's review where we are so far in the recovery process. We are BlackBerry abusers and overusers. We have used our BlackBerry smartphones at inappropriate times and in inappropriate places. We have acknowledged that that we need time away from our beloved messaging device, but we also need help. So, we have asked others to take it away for a short time, or we have asked for *interventions* to help us curtail our corrupt behavior.

" My 5-Year-Old Son

I try not to check my BlackBerry too much outside of work because my five-year old son said I pay more attention to it than him.

—Anonymous "

And so we come to the Step 8 on the road to BlackBerry recovery. In the traditional 12-step program, this is where we make a list of the people we have harmed and resolve to make amends for our bad behavior. It is easy to just shrug this one off and say, "Nobody gets hurt by my BlackBerry use." We can also rationalize our use of the device and say, "I'm working when I use it; I'm making a living for me and my family." The truth is, we can rationalize all we want. But if we spend too much time with our fingers on the keys, then we are taking time away from things, and the people around us that are far more important.

BlackBerry in Balance?
Who is more important to you?
What signals are you sending?

People Elsewhere

People Here

?

66 **BlackBerry at Funeral**

My mother passed away in January of this year, and in the limo ride to the grave site, my brother was so addicted to his BlackBerry that he used it the whole ride. His wife had to finally take it from him at the gravesite to ensure that he didn't look at it or get tempted to reply during the service.

My brother loved our mom, but just can't put the darn thing down for 15 minutes. He never established boundaries for its use, and he tends to have a personality anyway that always does things to an extreme or at a real intense level.

Boundaries and moderation in all things is a core life lesson that has been lost in our fast-food, drive-through, open 24/7, everything-has-to-be-convenient-and-immediately-accessible society. This addiction shouldn't really be a surprise. It is what is marketed to us as cool and valuable.

—Desires to be Anonymous 99

Using your BlackBerry during a funeral, memorial, or other service is an extreme example of ignoring the feelings of others. But such an example does help us put BlackBerry use and abuse into perspective.

Let's take a look back at some of the questions we answered in Chapter 5: "Am I a BlackBerry Abuser?" Our answers in that chapter might give us a clue about who we might actually be hurting with our bad BlackBerry behavior. One question asked in the list of questions was this: "Do you ever sneak away from groups to use your BlackBerry without anyone knowing?" Now, imagine that you are the person with whom you were having a conversation. There you are, engaged in dialogue with a friend or colleague, and all of the sudden they walk away—possibly in mid-sentence. Worse, you imagine you see this friend or colleague take out his BlackBerry and check for messages or email. What message does that send to you, the person left standing there? Can you possibly feel anything other than unimportant, ignored and even abandoned? How much did this person think about your feelings when he just walked away to check his BlackBerry.

What you feel now is the same feeling you inspire in others when you do similar things.

TIP: Place your BlackBerry far enough away from your bed so you can't reach it without getting up.

Here's another question we asked in Chapter 5 was this: "Do you have to check your BlackBerry before bed and immediately upon waking?"

Martin writes: I do this quite often. Now, I don't feel so badly about this if my wife is still sleeping. I am great at offering rational explanations: "I am part of a small company with clients around the world." It sounds convincing and even makes sense, but the truth is, it is just habit to check my email in this fashion. I want to see what I missed while I was sleeping. Maybe a new sale came in from the web site? Maybe our amazon.com ranking went up over night for our other books? Sometimes, I do want to get a jump on my busy day. However, if my wife is awake, I owe it to her to be attentive for the few minutes we have before she goes running off to work. I can usually wait an hour before reading my email and suffer only a minimal impact.

Concerned Bystanders

Sometimes BlackBerry users and abusers are approached by those around them with concerns about their BlackBerry overuse. Let's look at a few examples from Made Simple Learning customers and others.

 Quotes from Concerned Bystanders

My husband threatens to take it away all the time.

—Helen Ann R.

People tell me they're concerned all the time! I'm told I should seek a BlackBerry therapist.

—Lenny M.

My wife constantly tells me she's concerned.

—Jonathan D.

My wife was always complaining that I was on that thing all the time. So I bought her a BlackBerry, and it worked. Got her!

—Oscar M.

My family and friends have approached me about my BlackBerry use, and I have been asked many times to leave it at home or in the car while attending an event, so that I can give my full attention.

—Moe

My wife will ask me if I could ever watch a TV show without my BlackBerry in my hand. I tell her, "I don't think so."

—Ed H.

My girlfriend and I used to get into constant arguments about my BlackBerry. She often got frustrated when we would be watching a movie or talking. This all changed the day we got her a BlackBerry, too. Now we both share in the addiction!

—Super moderator paulbblc from the BlackBerryForums

I have had my BlackBerry for about two weeks, and my girlfriend hates the thing. I'm always on it, and so on. So I told her she could use it for a day. Well, when it came time for me to get my phone back, she wouldn't return it. We had to go get her a BlackBerry, as well!

—Greg8700G, BlackBerryForums.com Member

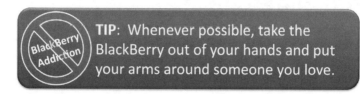

TIP: Whenever possible, take the BlackBerry out of your hands and put your arms around someone you love.

Most of us would scoff at the notion that our BlackBerry and, consequently, our email, is more important than our families and the ones we love. Yet, at times, our behavior says otherwise. When we reach for the BlackBerry instead of our spouse or partner, we inadvertently send the message that our work or even our 'Berry is what is most important to us, instead of those people right in front of us. Whenever possible, remember to take the BlackBerry out of your hands and put your arms around the ones you love.

You might also remember this question from the quiz in Chapter 5: "Have you ever checked your BlackBerry while at a meal with others?"

My guess is that many of us have engaged in this behavior from time to time. We may have dealt with why we engage in this behavior, but now we need to look at the consequences of our actions. In this scenario, we don't walk away. Nor do we sneak into the restroom to check our email. Rather, we take out our BlackBerry (or hide it under the table) and just ignore the people who are with us.

Again, we can rationalize this by saying: "Hey, the guy across the table has been doing this all night." So what? We should know better. Even if the conversation is boring, you are interacting with live human beings. You are engaging in social relationships, and those should be the priority of the moment.

Whether it is our own feeling of self-importance, our arrogance, our insecurities, or just plain rudeness, we should know better than to do this. These acts send a clear message to our friends and associates that they are just not as important as the new newsletter from www.CrackBerry.com or the email from our accountant.

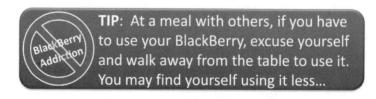

TIP: At a meal with others, if you have to use your BlackBerry, excuse yourself and walk away from the table to use it. You may find yourself using it less…

Missed a Big Hit at Baseball

I remember a couple of years ago, when I went to my son's baseball games. While it was true that I took time away from work to go to the field, sometimes three or four days a week, I was really there to see him. Too often, I took out my BlackBerry and did work, checked email, or simply surfed the Web when I got bored.

On one occasion, I was checking an insignificant email when my son got to the plate. This time he had a beautiful hit. When he got to first base, he looked over at me and saw me in the BlackBerry prayer position. I looked up and caught his eye as he stood on the base—but he and I both realized that I had missed his hit. I felt horrible. I felt like a jerk and a bad father.

—Gary Mazo

My guess is that we all have had moments like these, moments we that were lost and we can never have back because we were so engrossed in our BlackBerry smartphones. Shame on us!

Sometimes the BlackBerry ultimatum can arise: choose me or choose your BlackBerry. To the non-BlackBerry user, this ultimatum would likely swing towards the human side. To a BlackBerry addict, the choice might not favor the human side (see the story, "Berry vs. Boyfriend: Who Wins?").

Could we be in **denial** about our BlackBerry **Abuses?**

❝ Berry vs. Boyfriend: Who Wins?

So, I was dating this guy for about three months, and it was just getting serious. He was perfect: smart, efficient, practical, savvy, and best of all, always available. His name was 'Berry, which is short for BlackBerry. It was a perfect relationship. But, there came a point where 'Berry lacked the ability to give me the emotional attention that I needed. As much as I enjoyed sleeping next to 'Berry, with him on my night stand and me in bed, one can only wish for an in-bed companion. Which brings us to Derek.

Derek was the type of guy who would always open doors for you. He was the type to always make sure he let you know he was thinking of you every day. He was, all-in-all, a very nice guy and a very good catch. On the downside, he wasn't very tech savvy. The man had a Motorola Razor and thought it was groundbreaking. He was the guy that always forgot to charge his cell phone at night or left it at home and was able to go a whole work day without his phone by his side. Clearly, he didn't have the same relationship with his mobile device that 'Berry and I had.

I like to give people a good look into my life when they are about to enter it. So, during our first date, I put out a much-needed warning: I am reliable on my BlackBerry, but I have really bad phone etiquette. Of course, at the time this did not faze him. But I don't think he knew the severity of the BlackBerry disease that I had. It was his own fault for not realizing it was a serious thing. Why else would I feel the need to bring it up on a first date?

We were well into our fourth week of dating when I landed a new job at a high profile tech company here in Seattle. At this point, both Derek and I knew how we felt about each other—well as much as you know after four weeks together, anyway. We were having a nice dinner, when...

> **buzz buzz buzz**
> **typing typing typing**
> *"Sorry. Work," I said mid-email.*
> *"Yeah, but do you have to answer it at dinner?"*
> *"Yeah, it is kind of my job."*
> **buzz buzz buzz**

typing typing typing
"Really, you can't answer that later?" he asked as it became increasingly clear his dinner was slowly but surely being ruined.
buzz buzz buzz
buzz buzz buzz
buzz buzz buzz

This man then reaches over and takes 'Berry into custody.
Now, I want you to take into consideration that we are at a very nice restaurant. This is a place that he has wanted to take me for a while. So, yes, I felt bad for doing this, but A) this is my job and B) this is 'Berry we are talking about!

Some BlackBerry demon came over me, and I don't know what happened. I stood up, threw my napkin at him, grabbed my phone, and stormed out. All the while, I was saying some highly inappropriate things, such as "You are lucky there are witnesses around, or else your hands would not be capable of grabbing anything else for a very long time."

Needless to say, that was the very last time I saw him, talked to him, or even uttered his name until now.

True BlackBerry addiction overcomes the rules of attraction. This story does have a happy ending.

'Berry and I lived happily ever after.

— *Tristan* "

Sometimes, bystanders of BlackBerry addiction are created not by gross overuse of the device, but the lack of BlackBerry use altogether. No story can illustrate this better than that of one user who caused a full airplane of passengers to suffer because of his BlackBerry needs (see the story, "Frequent Flyer's Fiasco/Stand-by Hell").

Frequent Flyer's Fiasco/Stand-by Hell

It was Easter weekend, and I made the mistake of agreeing to travel from Seattle down to Southern California to visit my parents on a cheap stand-by flight. I figured if I got to the airport early enough (5 AM), I would be able to score the first flight out. Boy was I wrong. So wrong!

I was getting passed over on flight after flight. Not only was it Easter weekend, but it was also Spring break. It never really occurred to me that California is a Spring break getaway because I was born and raised in Southern California. At this point, I was able to catch a flight down to San Francisco in hopes that it would be easy to catch two shorter flights than one longer flight. Once again, I was wrong!

I spent about seven hours trying to get onto a flight in Seattle, and now I was going on my sixth hour doing the same in San Francisco. At this point, it is safe to say that I was delirious. I had basically overdosed on Starbucks and fast food. Every hour, I ran to a different gate, just to get turned down.

It had now come down to the point where if I didn't make this last flight, I would be staying the night in the San Francisco Airport. This would be the last flight to Southern California, and there were no more flights back to Seattle.

I remember the stomach-turning feeling I had while I was waiting to hear my name called to board the plane. And then, finally, I heard my name. I jumped up, grabbed my carry on, and boarded the plane.

The door was now closed on the airplane. The flight attendant had just finished making sure everyone was seated and securely fastened in. I reached for my BlackBerry to turn it to flight mode—and realized it was nowhere to be found. I'd left it at my seat in the airport!

My first reaction was to hit the call button. As soon as I realized that was not going to work, I unbuckled my seat belt, flung my body to a standing position, and started yelling, "I'm up! I am standing up!" That sure got me a lot of attention. The flight attendant came over, and I explained to her that I left my BlackBerry on my seat at the gate. She continued to tell me that there was no way I could run out and get it because the doors had already been closed. I told her to let me off immediately. She finally agreed to meet me half way. She checked whether someone in the airport could run out to my former seat, grab my BlackBerry, and then pass it to the captain through the cockpit window. To me, this sounded like the perfect plan!

By now, the passengers were wondering why weren't moving. I was starting to calm down because I felt my BlackBerry would be safe. I was just starting to relax when I heard:

BING
"Sorry for the inconvenience; a young gentleman has left his BlackBerry in the gate, and he has requested for us to obtain it for him. It is getting passed through the cockpit; we apologize for the 20 minute delay."

The flight attendant was putting me on blast! I couldn't believe it!

Now, let me explain to you the horror and sweet joy getting my BlackBerry was. Every row this flight attendant passed caused people to turn their heads, so people could catch a glimpse of this young gentleman who delayed the plane. By the time I had my BlackBerry in my hand, I also had every pair of eyes shooting rays of hatred from their pupils. I had found the most effective way to make new travel friends!

—Tristan L. 🙾

What's really amazing about this story is that flight attendants and pilots realized the vital importance of the BlackBerry to this passenger. I'd venture to argue that if Tristan had left some other phone or smartphone, or maybe even an iPhone in the airport, the plane would have taken off without delay. A BlackBerry on the other hand? Better hold the flight! Better to inconvenience and delay a plane load of passengers rather than have a BlackBerry addict forced to go cold turkey on his flight!

The story shows us that we are all BlackBerry bystanders in this world; there is no escaping the phenomenon. Sometimes, even the BlackBerry addict will become a BlackBerry bystander (see the story, "Kevin's Missing Curve").

66 Kevin's Missing Curve

I experienced the frustration of losing my BlackBerry firsthand in 2007, when the BlackBerry Curve was first released. I had seen a sneak peek of RIM's newest phone at the company's annual partner show (Wireless Enterprise Symposium) in Orlando, Florida. The Curve was amazing and sure to be a big hit. However, when it came time to release the phone to the world, the 02 wireless network in the UK was first to get it.

AT&T was scheduled to launch a few weeks later. My BlackBerry addiction was a bit out of hand, so I couldn't wait to get my hands on RIM's newest release, and I forced a friend in Europe to buy the phone for me the day it was released and then ship it out to me in Canada.

The online tracking said that the phone left for Canada, but the local UPS office never received it. My Curve didn't arrive. Obviously, it's wrong to point fingers because even UPS' investigation turned up nothing. However, I'm pretty sure there is one more BlackBerry addict in the world today, thanks to my device that never arrived.

—Kevin Michaluk 99

Exercise: List Your Own BlackBerry Bystanders

At this point, you're ready to list all those people whom you may have offended or hurt or could have hurt (but luckily did not) while using your BlackBerry in an abusive or rude manner.

(Don't be shy; feel free to add more lines if you need them!)

1.

_____

_____

_____

_____

_____

_____

_____

_____

_____

_____

_____

"Scooping BlackBerry Poop"

In this chapter, we will walk you through Step 9 of overcoming BlackBerry addiction: making amends to those we've wronged.

> ### Step 9:
> #### Make Amends to Our BlackBerry Bystanders

Step 9: Make amends to our BlackBerry bystanders. We will make amends to those whom we have wronged by our BlackBerry abuses; we will "Scoop our BlackBerry Poop."

In other words, it's time to do the hard work of not just recognizing our wrongs, but also addressing them and righting them.

At the end of the previous chapter, we identified those whom we have hurt. We also acknowledged more bad behavior and resolved to make amends. Well, talk is great, but it is also cheap. On our road to BlackBerry recovery, we must now clean up the mess we've made. Step 9 of the official 12-step program requires that we to make amends, except when doing so would cause injury or unnecessary pain. This chapter deals with cleaning up our BlackBerry mess.

In the previous chapter, we shared some personal stories of the BlackBerry messes we have created from time to time. For example, Gary shared the story of his BlackBerry use at everything from his son's baseball game to a dinner out with friends. He can't get those moments back. However, it is possible that Gary was able to rationalize his behavior (given that he works in the BlackBerry business), but we all know the truth.

The simplest, but most difficult thing to do seems to be to apologize directly for our bad behavior. This is only one way—one small way—of cleaning up the mess. We begin with the ones we love, the *innocent bystanders* we spoke of in previous chapters. Gary can certainly say "I'm sorry" to his son for missing his hit.

I'm Sorry...

The look in Gary's son's eyes was one of disappointment on that day, and no father likes to disappoint his kids. So, Gary can let him know that in the future he will to try to keep his BlackBerry in the car and not even bring it to the game or whatever other activity his kids might be participating in. Gary will focus his attention on his kids. If Gary needs to make a call (which sometimes does happen), he can go back to the car and not pretend to watch. In today's world, sometimes it is important to be reachable. However, it isn't always essential to take every call and read every email immediately.

Is it really **essential** that I have my **BlackBerry** now?

TIP: Turn off vibrate & ringer for new Email so you aren't tempted to grab for your BlackBerry at every message. (Profiles > Advanced > Edit Messages)

Remember the situation from the last chapter, where you were checking email under the table when you thought no one was watching? Or perhaps you are someone who checks the BlackBerry as the last thing you do at night and the first thing in the morning. If so, you might tell your significant other, "I'm sorry that I do this." Maybe you can resolve to keep your BlackBerry somewhere else. If you need the phone near you in case of emergency, resolve to only answer important phone calls.

Fortunately, the technology of the BlackBerry itself can actually help you clean up your mess. Not only can you resolve to not check your email before bed, but you can set the preferences of your BlackBerry to only check for email during certain hours. If you feel that you might be expecting an important text message from one of your kids, you can give the SMS messages a different look and feel. For example, you might give it a custom ring tone or adjust the LED notification. If you're expecting a call from the boss, you could give her a unique caller tone, so you can easily identify that call you may need to answer.

If you take your BlackBerry to bed with you each night, don't think you're alone. It's a common occurrence. RIM now has a feature in the BlackBerry operating system software called **Bedside** mode. When you place your BlackBerry in the charging pod accessory, it automatically enters bedside mode and displays a clock on the screen. You can fine-tune the **Bedside** mode settings, such as disabling alerts from coming through while you're sleeping (or even shutting off the device radio altogether). If you are unsure of how to do any of these tasks, just visit www.crackberrybook.com or check the forums at www.crackberry.com for easy solutions that can help you.

On a truly serious note, one area where you really do hurt people with your BlackBerry use is when you text or read and reply to email while driving. Please don't ever do it; make that resolution now. If it is so essential to get a message to someone, there are some great third-party software programs than can convert voice to text and then deliver emails and text messages. **DriveSafe.ly**, **Vlingo**, **Jott and Nuance**, and **Voice on the Go** come to mind as a few examples that might work. Or better yet, pull over to the side of the road if you really need to focus on an activity other than driving!

TIP: Use voice-activated software if you absolutely need to use your BlackBerry in your vehicle. Examples: www.jott.com, www.voiceonthego.com

We tell you all about these tips in our books and on our web sites. Injuring or, worse, killing someone because you were texting or emailing while driving is one mess that you won't be able to clean up, and it is completely avoidable.

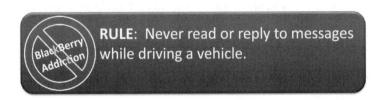

RULE: Never read or reply to messages while driving a vehicle.

Some of the members and users of www.CrackBerry.com have shared the following stories with us.

❝ Jam on My BlackBerry while at a Red Light

I'm guilty of checking email, messaging, and placing calls while driving. It's pretty hard to type while driving, so I keep the sentences shorter. But if I'm at a stoplight, I do the "Flight of the Bumblebee" with my thumbs to shoot out tons of text to the person I'm responding to. Personally, I think I can type pretty quickly on the BlackBerry; that teenage girl who won the SMS Text Messaging speed competition better watch out!

— tbetts1982, CrackBerry.com Member

❝ Use BlackBerry AutoText to Reply in Car

If my son is in the car with me, I will have him check the message for me. If I am alone, sometimes I will send a quick reply at a stoplight.

Just yesterday I made a new AutoText: ppp, which translates to this: "Driving, will reply soon." I drive a six-speed, and I am not skilled enough to text and shift at the same time.

— MiniBlackBerry, CrackBerry.com Member

TIP: Ask someone else in the vehicle with you to check your messages and read them to you. The passenger can also type a reply, if required.

" BlackBerry on Wheel, Typing Next to A Police Officer

I'm in bumper to bumper traffic most of the time driving home, so I get about 25-50 emails sent out on the way home. I also read RSS feeds, SMS Text, and so on. I've done this for years, and my BlackBerry is always at the top of the steering wheel. While I'm typing with one hand, I can see the road, as well as what I'm typing as I drive. I've done it while cops were driving next to me and behind me, and I've never had an issue.

—audit , CrackBerry.com Member

Often, when we think of CrackBerry addiction, we think of the BlackBerry user herself as being the burdened individual. But, as with any addiction, most CrackBerry addicts fail to realize their actions may be out of the norm. Tom's story of lunch with an addicted co-worker portrays a common BlackBerry Addict occurrence (see the story, "He Stopped in mid-Story to Use His BlackBerry").

📖 He Stopped in mid-Story to Use His BlackBerry

First of all, I'm not a BlackBerry owner, nor have I have ever used one. However, I work in an office environment where there are a few people who love their CrackBerry. Usually it doesn't bother me at all. But other times I feel jealous because they can check and respond to their email while on the go, while I can't).

Usually, I'm quite tolerant of others. But today I observed some disturbing behavior by my fellow co-worker while we were having lunch. For lunch, four of us decided to go out for sushi, and my co-worker proudly placed his CrackBerry on the table. Ok, no big deal. During lunch, he would periodically check his 'Berry for new messages (or whatever he was looking at), and this didn't bother me either.

But finally, he did something that really did disturb me. He was talking to the rest of the attentive group around the table and was in the middle of a story saying, "I know this military guy..." Then he glances at his 'Berry and says "Oh oh." Next, he starts furiously reading his screen without ever excusing himself, leaving everyone else around the table dumbfounded. I think this person needs rehab!

—Tom, CrackBerry.com Member 📖

One thing that is clear is that there is plenty of BlackBerry Poop to be scooped. Many a BlackBerry user (and most BlackBerry abusers) have hurt people or annoyed others with their insensitivity when using their BlackBerries. Have you ever been given the "evil eye" at the movies or in a restaurant? Have you ever had your spouse or significant other, or perhaps your kids just lose it with you because you were so intent on answering the email or checking something on line on your BlackBerry?

You are making great progress through this book. But now it's time to go back and try to fix some of the damage you've caused. It's time to make amends, to do the right thing and clean up your mess.

Please use the checklist That follows to help you complete this important step in your BlackBerry recovery.

Exercise: Create a Checklist for Apologizing to Your BlackBerry Bystanders

Please rewrite your bystanders list from the previous chapter, and then check or cross off the names of people as you complete your apologies.

☐ _____

☐ _____

☐ _____

☐ _____

☐ _____

☐ _____

☐ _____

☐ _____

☐ _____

☐ _____

☐ _____

"BlackBerry Etiquette"

In this chapter, we will walk you through Step 10 of overcoming your BlackBerry addiction: adhering to basic rules intended to keep your BlackBerry use (and abuse) in check.

Step 10:
Tirelessly Adhere to BlackBerry Etiquette Rules

Step 10: Tirelessly adhere to BlackBerry etiquette rules. We resolve to live by the BlackBerry Etiquette Rules. When we break them, we will work hard to fix our ways.

In other words, we resolve to turn off the BlackBerry during all meetings, classes, presentations, weddings, and funerals. We will also refrain from using our BlackBerry during dinner, while at the movies with our significant other, or in the bedroom.

We may even need to detox from the BlackBerry for a short period, until we can learn to use them without hurting ourselves or others.

Our journey has taken us to the Step 10 chapter. Traditionally, this is the step where we establish a personal practice that helps us take a constant personal inventory and take corrective measures before we veer off our path. For BlackBerry users and abusers, this means that we must resolve to live by several interventions, rules, and tips, which we'll cover momentarily.

BlackBerry Abuse Interventions and Etiquette Rules

The authors are grateful to Made Simple Learning customer, KC, who provided many of the interventions and rules that follow. We've modified these only slightly, to format them for inclusion in this book. It's possible that we can all adapt these practices to help us step away from the BlackBerry and maintain a sense of balance in our lives:

Intervention #1: Check the BlackBerry at the door when you arrive home and do not look at it until after dinner.

Intervention #2: Leave the BlackBerry in the car when you are attending a family event or kid's activity. Focus on the family; all email, BBM, and other messaging can wait at least one hour.

Intervention #3: No electronic devices at or near the dinner table during *any* meals. Thus, kids can't bring Game Boys, and mom or dad can't bring their BlackBerry smartphones.

Intervention #4: Do not use the BlackBerry while driving any vehicle; if you must use the BlackBerry, then pull over and stop. Note that a Bluetooth Headset for calls is permissible.

Intervention #5: Do not use your BlackBerry to send or reply to messages after 10:00 PM. When emailing at night, exhaustion can cause come through as a disrespectful tone. We are also more inclined to miscommunicate. We all need time to turn off our brains and rest.

Intervention # 6: If you follow the aforementioned five interventions, others will learn that you are not available 24 / 7, and their expectations for replies will be more appropriate and supportive of you having a real life.

A Made Simple Learning customer points out the benefits of following these interventions in the story, "Achieve Balance with Interventions."

" Achieve Balance with Interventions

Co-workers, friends, and family know when I can be reached, as well as my boundaries for a response. I set aside time with my family, and my family and I get to enjoy life a little bit.

It took me a while to discipline myself this way. But I started with an email and voicemail boundaries message to all that stated the points of the preceding paragraph. My boss, co-workers, business colleagues, spouse, kids, and friends all responded positively. Today, reply expectations are balanced with a personal life and family time.

—KC **"**

Addiction Avoidance Tips

Addiction avoidance tips are not as strict as the interventions; however, such tips can help nudge you into more responsible BlackBerry use:

Tip: Place your BlackBerry far enough away from your bed that you can't reach it without getting up.

Tip: Use **Bedside** mode or manually turn your BlackBerry to **Off** at night, or use the **Auto Off** feature (**Options ➤ Auto On/Off**).

Tip: Whenever possible, take the BlackBerry out of your hands and put your arms around someone you love. (Whenever possible and appropriate, make that someone the person who bought you this book!)

Tip: At a meal with others, excuse yourself and walk away from the table if you find you must use your BlackBerry. You may find yourself using your BlackBerry less.

Tip: Turn off vibrate and ringer for new email, so you aren't tempted to grab for your BlackBerry at every message. Do this by selecting **Sound Profiles > Edit Profiles > Select a Profile > Edit various types of alerts (Email, Calendar, BBM, etc.)** You can also disable the red blinking LED light too while you're at it.

Tip: Plug in your BlackBerry for nightly charging in a room other than your bedroom. That way, you won't be tempted to turn it on in the middle of the night!

Tip: Ask someone else in the vehicle with you to check your messages and read them to you. The passenger can also type a reply, if required.

Tip: Use voice-activated software if you absolutely need to use your BlackBerry in your vehicle. Examples of such software include **Vlingo, drivesafe.ly, Jott** and **Voice On the Go**.

Tip: Try to avoid sending a quick message reply anytime day or night. You are *setting expectations* that you will always do this!

Tip: *Stop* and *look* around you. Will your colleagues, friends, or family be afraid to approach you because you seem "too busy with your BlackBerry?"

Tip: When on vacation, use an out-of-office reply to colleagues whom you will not respond to by email until you return. Also, provide an emergency contact person (not you), if necessary.

Tip: Try to setting your BlackBerry down for 15 minutes. Next, try setting it down for 20 minutes, and then 30 minutes or more. Try to wean yourself off the device slowly.

Tip: Set your personal appointments (e.g., spouse, kids, and friends) on your BlackBerry with equal priority to your work appointments. And keep them!

Tip: When you're on a bike ride, set your **Sound Profile** on your BlackBerry to do nothing for email, SMS, and calendar alarms. Leave the phone on if you need people to keep in touch with you.

If someone gets used to us replying within 10 minutes at any time, day or night, he will come to expect *such prompt responses. If someone gets used to us staying up late checking email, they will send you email at all hours of the day and expect a quick reply.*

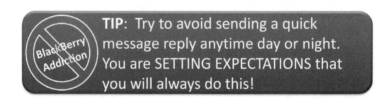

TIP: Try to avoid sending a quick message reply anytime day or night. You are SETTING EXPECTATIONS that you will always do this!

Here is another set of rules, courtesy of a kind user at www.CrackBerry.com (see the sidebar, "Top Ten Rules to Live By."

" Top Ten BlackBerry Rules to Live By

10. Never use your BlackBerry at a family function.

9. Never use your BlackBerry on a date with your spouse or loved one.

8. Never use your BlackBerry while operating a motor vehicle.

7. Never use your BlackBerry in the restroom.

6. Never use your BlackBerry in a movie theater.

5. Never use your BlackBerry at one of your children's concerts.

4. Never use your BlackBerry in a hospital.

3. Never use your BlackBerry at church.

2. Never use your BlackBerry in a meeting at work.

And the #1 rule for BlackBerry use: Rules 10 through 2 are null and void if you think you can get away with it!

—Chad, CrackBerry.com Member "

We need to go above and beyond these rules. We also need to make some lifestyle change,s so we can continually practice good BlackBerry etiquette and restore some balance to our frenetic lives.

Top 10 BlackBerry Productivity Myths Busted

One way to establish the extended rules of behavior it to bust some of the popular BlackBerry Myths that exist, myths that drive us to rationalize the behavior and actions that got us to buy this book in the first place (we, the authors, would like to add that we are most grateful that you did). The top 10 most popular BlackBerry myths are as follows:

1. I'm more successful because I'm available 24 / 7 with my BlackBerry!

2. Always using my BlackBerry during "downtime" makes me more productive.

3. If I respond with short messages (email or text) immediately, I'm more productive.

4. It's OK to use my BlackBerry at a stoplight.

5. That slight pain in my hand is nothing!

6. Multitasking on my BlackBerry makes me much more productive.

7. It's OK to use my BlackBerry in front of my children and spouse; they're doing something else anyways.

8. It's OK to use my BlackBerry in the bathroom.

9. It's OK to use my BlackBerry at the dinner table (or restaurant).

10. I'm more productive because I respond to email during boring presentations or business meetings.

Now, if you have been reading this book closely and thinking seriously about what we say, then you will recognize that each myth is just that: a myth, or rationalization for bad behavior. The only way to dispel these myths and see the truth is to make a conscious effor to change your attitude, perception, and behavior.

Rationalizing Our BlackBerry Use

As we have been discussing in this book, we are great at rationalizing our BlackBerry addiction. For example, we say things like the following:

- If I am working all the time, then that must mean I am a good provider, husband, mother, and so on.

- If I am working all the time with my BlackBerry, then I am not doing the devil's work. Idle hands make idle minds.

- I must keep working with my BlackBerry to prove my worth to the world. I am only what I accomplish in this life. I have no worth outside what I accomplish.

In the words of Sigmund Freud: "This is a load of crap—a huge pile of BlackBerry poop that needs to be scooped." Ok, maybe Freud didn't say that. But if he had been alive during the days of BlackBerry overuse, he might have. There is so much more to life than work.

Do you know why work is called *work*? Because all the other four letter words were taken! There is a wonderful Cherokee Expression on the "Meaning of Life."

> *When you were born, you cried and the world rejoiced. Live your life so when you die, the world cries and you rejoice.*
>
> *—a Cherokee Expression*

A personal favorite statement on the purpose of life comes from the incredibly simple philosophy of the Dalai Lama:

> *What is the purpose of life? I believe that the purpose of life is to be happy.*
>
> *—the Dalai Lama*

Now, we need to ask ourselves whether using our BlackBerry in ways that bring pain to others is really what brings us happiness? If you answered "Yes, this is what brings me happiness," then please re-read this book, beginning with Chapter 1. We will be waiting right here for you when you finally "get it" and return to this point in the book.

Early on in this book, we talked about needing to be masters of our BlackBerry, not the other way around. At this stage on our path towards recovery, it's espeically important that we be in control of the 'Berry and not be controlled by it.

The Table Analogy

Basic etiquette tells us that there is a simple way to set a table properly. We put forks on the left, and we put knives and spoons on the right. Sometimes, we get fancy and put little forks to the left of bigger forks; we might also do the same with spoons. But these issues are not as important.

What is important is that there are certain acceptable, societal norms for setting the table, and the manners we bring to the table reflect on our basic etiquette and decency. For example, we should avoid slurping our soup (except in Asia), keeping our elbows off the table, chewing with our mouth open, and so on.

The same holds true for using our BlackBerry at the table. Typically, a BlackBerry should go to the left of the smallest fork (if space permits) or in the space below the silverware. A BlackBerry should be turned so that the red light faces you and no one else. A BlackBerry should also be put into **Silent** mode when at the table. When the red light goes off, try not to look at it. Instead, just let it blink and wait until someone at the table says, "Hey, I think you have an email." That acknowledgment will give you permission to cradle your BlackBerry in your hand and check your email.

"Conscious Contact or Constant Contact?"

In this chapter, we will walk you through Step 11 of overcoming your BlackBerry addiction: setting priorities for our BlackBerry use.

> ### Step 11:
> **Resolve to Reconnect With Others Around Us**

> ## When you are on your BlackBerry and doing something else, have you noticed that both suffer?

Step 11: Resolve to reconnect with others around us. We resolve to reconnect and have *conscious contact* with those directly around us, rather than *constant contact* with those on the other end of our BlackBerry.

In other words, it's time to rely less on our beloved 'Berry for companionship, and more on the family and friends who figure most significantly in our lives.

Congratulations! You are making progress. You have identified bad behavior, you have resolved to make changes, you have reached out to those you have hurt, and you have begun to set a path upon which you can walk with your head up (not hunched over checking email.) You are almost ready to embark on a new way to live life, where you can be present for your loved ones and still enjoy the benefits of your BlackBerry—in moderation.

In the traditional 12-step program, Step 11 of the recovery process speaks about making conscious contact and using prayer and meditation to help ground us and connect us to our own definition of our higher power. When we do this, we realize that there are things much more important than us and way more important than our BlackBerry. These things can offer us guidance and give our lives meaning. As we have pointed out in previous chapters, we are very quick to rationalize bad behavior. However, we do realize that sometimes BlackBerry overuse does reflect poorly on us, even in the professional world with which we so desperately try to stay connected.

When you are on your BlackBerry and doing something else, have you noticed that both suffer? Studies have shown that multitasking can cut down on the pleasure that a person takes from the process of doing activities when more than one activity is done at a time. Studies have also shown that multitasking may decrease efficiency because the brain is not able to give adequate attention to any one of the many tasks that are competing for its time.

The authors want to give special thanks to business and life coach Martha Young, JD/MBA, for the content that follows. Martha works with lawyers and business professionals. She contributed to this book, and she can help you to kick your BlackBerry addiction as a part of reaching greater goal,s such as business growth and closer relationships. To learn more about her work, go to www.cleardialogue.com or email her at martha@cleardialogue.com.

> **Multitasking may even decrease efficiency because the brain is not able to give adequate attention to any one of the many tasks that are competing for its time.**

The simple techniques that follow can help you connect you to your higher power, ground you, and, ultimately make you more effective and productive:

Meditation: Take five minutes a day in the morning to center your mind. If you are using a BlackBerry because you think it gives you an edge in keeping connected to your customers, then consider focusing on how you will provide the best service for your customers and meet their needs. Go over the faces of your customers as you meditate in silence and think about how you might serve them best. With quiet time and clear thinking, you may be able to connect with ideas that will benefit you and your customers. The BlackBerry is not the only way to achieve your goal. In this case, what may be most important is the quality or type of your communication, not its quantity or speed.

Affirmations: Consider whether your customers may be able to prosper and while you succeed whether you check your BlackBerry 5 times a day or 50. You might want to try this out. Try going for a week where you check your BlackBerry only 5 times per day. Say to yourself whenever you have the urge to check your BlackBerry, "My customers and I are prospering whether I check my BlackBerry or not."

Distract yourself. Put music on, take a bike ride, hike to the top of a mountain, work out, get away from thinking about work. Turn your BlackBerry off and engage in some activity that takes all of your concentration and that you enjoy.

Prayer: We all joke about the *BlackBerry Prayer Position*: head bowed, hands together in front of your face, and the solemn expression. Of course, what you are really doing is using your thumbs to type the email (even in a place of worship.) So, here is something else to try: Assume the same position, sans BlackBerry. Whatever your understanding of your higher power may be, try to connect with that power through dialogue with your thoughts, instead of through your thumbs.

Helping You Reflect on Your BlackBerry Addiction

This chapter is all about *coming clean* and connecting with the things that really matter. Take a few minutes and reflect carefully on the following questions:

- Think about a time when you lied about using your BlackBerry. What was happening? To whom did you lie? Why did you lie? What were you afraid would happen if you didn't lie?

- Sit with this knowledge for a moment. Many times it makes sense to lie because you fear some sort of punishment if you were to tell the truth. Children who get caught lying might get grounded or lose their allowance. What is the punishment you fear you might face if you told the truth about your BlackBerry use?

- Do you think your spouse or partner will criticize you? If this is true, we suggest that you come to some agreement with your partner, family, and friends about when it's OK or not OK to use your BlackBerry. Once you reach such agreement, it's important that you honor it and turn off your BlackBerry during those times when you've agreed not to use it.

This is similar to the *hospital approach*. You've probably seen the hospital signs that say, "No cell phone use." Similarly, airplanes do not allow cell phone use during flights. The issue is that the cell phone can actually interfere with the equipment in the hospital or on the airplane, and thus potentially endanger the lives or health of those around you.

Consider that your BlackBerry use could endanger the emotional health of your relationships. There is a cost to a relationship or family when one of the members is not fully present because she is checking email or answering cell phone calls. Over time, the BlackBerry user may not be asked to engage in some activities. Other family members may count on the BlackBerry user to give only part of their attention to the activity, so they may give up on them in little ways. For example, a child might see you at the kitchen table drinking coffee in the morning and using the BlackBerry, and thus refrain from approaching you to talk about something that is bothering him at school. The worst part: You may never know what conversations aren't happening because others have tuned you out, too.

Or, the potential future love of your life might see you on a park bench, but assume you are busy to talk and never approach you. Again, the costs here are often hidden; you may never know what you are missing out on, but your life will be less complete for it, nonetheless.

When she was young, Martin's youngest daughter learned how to let him know when she had had enough of him making calls, a technique she continues to use to this day. She will start screaming out, "No phone, no phone!" Martin is actually glad she does this. He says: "I will be afraid about the day when she stops doing this and just gives up on me as a playmate." You may have friends, family, and others who have given up on you because they never get all of your attention when you are glancing down at your BlackBerry.

Now, the news isn't all bad. There are great ways that you can use your BlackBerry to help you connect with what is truly important. If you are person of faith, there are free and pay versions of the Bible and other sacred literature that you can read on your BlackBerry. Or, you might find a meaningful Thought for the Day website and subscribe to a daily inspirational message.

Your BlackBerry can also be used as a tool for connecting in new ways to your loved ones (see the story, "Staying in Touch with My Dad").

66 Staying Better In Touch with My Dad

Well, my Dad recently got a BlackBerry, and I'm jealous. We got the BlackBerry Messenger set up for him, and now were PINing (i.e., sending BlackBerry-to-BlackBerry PIN text messages) each other. The ability to send quick messages back and forth is extremely cool. The nice thing is that we can stay in touch a little more easily because now we have the ability to send quick messages and emails to one another at any time. This helps us stay in touch better because there are times when phone calls are not appropriate, but emails or text messages are.

—*wxboss, CrackBerry.com Member* 99

The preceding story gives us a great concluding thought for this chapter. What better way to establish *conscious contact* with those we love than by buying them a BlackBerry? In fact, both Martin and Gary's fathers are now the proud owners of new BlackBerry smartphones and copies of our books. Kevin also hooked his mom up with a BlackBerry recently. This is her first cell phone ever, and the phone's **BlackBerry Messenger** program has brought them even closer together.

The truth is that there are more important things than our BlackBerry smartphones, and we all can find more time to spend with friends and family. It's also true that we can all do with a little less time opening what seem to be life-altering emails and spend more time meditating, praying, or conducting meaningful dialogue with those we love.

"Typing the Talk and Walking the Walk"

In this chapter, we will walk you through Step 12 of overcoming your BlackBerry addiction: acting responsibly and spreading the word.

Hmm...
Maybe I can
kick this habit
after all!

Step 12:
Resolve to be Responsible and Spread the Word

Step 12: Resolve to be responsible and spread the word. We resolve to stick to the rules and help other BlackBerry abusers learn and practice these rules of responsible BlackBerry Use. We promise to "Type the Talk" and "Walk the Walk." We encourage everyone we know to buy this book and learn the path to responsible BlackBerry use.

In other words, we have examined the roots of our BlackBerry addiction problems and resolved to do better. Now it's time to make that transition from imagining how to do better by implementing the techniques outlined in this book.

At this point, we need to walk the walk and talk the talk, as it were. We also need to help others who are still struggling with their BlackBerry use and abuse.

So here we are. We are ready to approach living with our BlackBerry in a new light. We have established a plan for healthy BlackBerry behavior, our old ways have been abandoned, and we'ere readey to chart a new path of BlackBerry use, one where we don't abuse the device. The traditional Step 12 in a 12-step program calls upon us to carry this message forth. It also calls on us to carry these principles into all aspects of our lives.

There is a progression to achieving good BlackBerry behavior. Please refer back to our "BlackBerry Etiquette Rules" list.

If BlackBerry use during meetings is a problem, try to either outlaw BlackBerry use during meetings, to define monetary fines for unauthorized BlackBerry use, or to set breaks every 30 minutes for people to check their BlackBerry smartphones.

BlackBerry Addiction Avoidance Tips

It doesn't matter whether we are the BlackBerry abuser or we employ, work for, live with, or are related to the BlackBerry abuser. We are all affected by BlackBerry misuse, and we all can help to initiate change. To that end, what follows are some guidelines that can help both the BlackBerry abuser and those around her to overcome her CrackBerry addiction.

Advice for Employers

Don't force your employees to be "on call" 24 hours a day just because they have a BlackBerry.

Advice for Parents

You need to set limits for your kids with respect to their BlackBerry use. Here are two key things you can do to encourage responsible BlackBerry use by your kids:

- Teach them to not respond to unsolicited email or text messages.

- Set basic rules, such as no texting at the table, no email while doing homework, and so on.

Advice for All BlackBerry Users

Finally, here is some general advice that all BlackBerry users would be wise to adopt:

- *Don't take yourself too seriously*: Yes, you have the coolest device around, but so what? Your device doesn't define you; you define it. So make your BlackBerry proud by behaving appropriately.

- *Be kind, courteous and respectful*: Don't talk loudly in public places, don't leave the table to answer an email, and don't even bring your BlackBerry to the table! Above all else, don't ever text or email while driving. Be sure to use a third-party voice-to-text program, if necessary.

- *Remember that your BlackBerry is a tool*: You are the device's master. It does what you want, not the other way around. If you let the BlackBerry control you, you're the one who ends up looking and acting like a tool!

Properly used, the BlackBerry is an amazing tool. You can use it to organize your life, schedule every moment of your time, keep all your contact information and personal data in one place, invite people to meetings, listen to music, watch videos, and so on. This is all in addition to using the device for its core functions such as checking and composing emails, text messages, and more.

Each of the authors of this book freely admits that he is guilty of BlackBerry overuse. Each of them also supports his families in whole or in part through BlackBerry-related career choices. Not one of them one disputes the superiority of the platform (OK, *other* people might make a case for some other phone from Cupertino, CA—but we know better) or the abilities of the BlackBerry to make people more productive. However, each of us has come to understand that, as with everything else, too much of a good thing can cease to be a good thing.

We encourage you to use your BlackBerry smartphones proudly and to celebrate the culture of which you are a part. We also encourage you to follow the steps in this book to text responsibly, talk respectfully, email courteously, and remember that there are places and times when using your BlackBerry is just inappropriate.

> ## The Responsible BlackBerry User Credo:
>
> **I promise not to use my BlackBerry in any situation that could harm myself or others – either in body or mind.**

We firmly believe that responsible BlackBerry use will enhance and restore balance to your life. We also believe that responsible BlackBerry use will foster harmony with those you love. If you feel yourself starting to slip and fall off the BlackBerry Wagon, then please review the earlier chapters in the book and work through the process again. You can also do the following:

Visit `www.crackberry.com` and join the CrackBerry rehab group in the community forums. Here you can gain strength from other recovered BlackBerry users and abusers.

Visit `www.crackberrybook.com` to sign up for the CrackBerry book email tips and tricks.

Our Final Thoughts

We hope you have enjoyed learning about ways that you can be more responsible in how you use your BlackBerry. We also hope it helps you achieve a better, more productive, and ultimately more satisfying personal and professional life. In this chapter, we'll touch on some final thoughts we'd like to share, including suggestions for getting the most out of both this book and your BlackBerry in general.

Gary's Final Thoughts

When I took the quiz in Chapter 5, I answered **Yes** to 17 of the questions. My wife, Gloria, thinks I really should have scored a 19! I have taken the tough step to admit that I have a problem, that I am a BlackBerry abuser. That said, I have resolved to make some changes.

One of the first changes that I've made relates to something I spoke of earlier in this book: I no longer use my BlackBerry as my music player on bike rides. Too often, a phone call would come in, and I would stop my ride and start working when I should have been relaxing. It was also rude to my riding partners. So, now I only bring the BlackBerry for "emergency purposes." I now put it in the pack under the seat and set the profile so it won't ring.

Another change that I've made is to leave my BlackBerry in the car when I go out to eat with my family or to the movies with my wife. It was too tempting to check email during the previews or when the teams changed sides. Invariably, this led to continued emails and then phone calls and ignoring my loved ones. I've been trying to make my off time sacred, I've trying out the notion that folks can wait a little while for receiving a response from me.

Kevin's Final Thoughts

When I initially took the quiz in Chapter 5, I answered **Yes** to 26 out of 27 questions. When you run a site like www.CrackBerry.com, I guess being a BlackBerry abuser is part of the job description. The question about whether I wished I could take the BlackBerry into the shower with me actually solicited the answer of **Other**. It was shortly after I got my BlackBerry that I started soaking in a bath tub instead; there's no need to stop using my device that way!

When I finally had the realization that BlackBerry addiction was a serious problem (the night I discovered my girlfriend was more into her BlackBerry than me), I finally decided to do something about my addiction. For me, it really came down to out-of-sight, out-of-mind. Still feeling naked without a BlackBerry nearby, I tricked myself by using the device's **Auto-Off** feature. I'd set the device to automatically turn off shortly past my bedtime and turn on again shortly before I woke up. This ensured a good night's sleep and curbed the temptation to wake up in the middle of the night and check out why the red light was blinking.

But after a while, the thought of having the phone turned off completely started to scare me. What if there were an emergency, and someone needed to call me? So, I created a custom profile for bedtime that left the ringer on, but silenced all other notifications. RIM employees must have been thinking the same thing because all new BlackBerry smartphones have a **Bedside** mode function built into the **Clock** application.

When going out to restaurants, I began leaving the device in the car. Similarly, I try to leave the BlackBerry in my locker when I visit the gym. When sitting at home and watching a movie, I began to leave my BlackBerry in the other room with the profile set to **Phone Only**. Baby steps! Regardless, with effort I have weaned myself from absolute dependence on the device, and now I score a controlled 6 on the BlackBerry Addiction quiz.

But once an addict, always an addict. The bad thing about addictions is that people are subject to relapse, and that's been an issue for me in this case. While I now have my BlackBerry use under control, it does take discipline and conscious effort to maintain control over the device. Every day is a struggle, and I've found responsible use to be a slippery slope. Given the chance, my addiction may slide out of control again. That said, I take it a day at a time, and I am much better off than I was thanks to the information, stories, and knowledge gained in working on this book.

Martin's Final Thoughts

After more than nine years of continuous BlackBerry use, I feel that I'm really starting to get my abuses under control—or maybe I just hide them better. I've been scolded enough by my family and friends that I now know how to put the BlackBerry in its proper place. To be honest, I have my share of relapses, especially when something exciting is going on at work or someone buys something from our web site.

I have done my best to never look at my BlackBerry when I'm reading books with our youngest daughter or tucking her into bed. I appreciate that it sends a bad signal! Now, I try to use my BlackBerry mostly when I'm alone or when I'm walking our dogs, Belle (a Black Lab), Wolfie (a long-haired Dachshund), and Pixie (a Labradoodle).

I don't think the dogs mind too much, but maybe they do. I'll have to look into their eyes next time I'm typing away on the BlackBerry around them.

In gathering stories and helping to write this book with Gary and Kevin, I've definitely learned to be more sensitive to those around me, especially with respect to the safety issues of using a mobile device while driving. I now realize that it requires constant vigilance to be a *responsible BlackBerry user* and live by the recommended rules, tips, and interventions.

Constant Effort

Congratulations! You've made it through this book. It might not have been easy to recognize just how impolite you were with regards to your BlackBerry use; however, you can rest assured that you are not alone. We are all in this together. In any case, we hope you have learned something substantial in reading this book. We also hope you have resolved how to make some genuine changes in your life with regards to your BlackBerry use.

You may have also realized that making real and lasting changes is difficult to do all alone. Lasting change requires both a constant, ongoing effort and help from your friends, family, colleagues, and your higher power, whatever form that might take.

If you have learned something and want to make some changes immediately, keep reading. If you just want to fuel your addiction and learn even more cool stuff to do with your BlackBerry, then head on over to www.madesimplelearning.com and check out our BlackBerry books and videos. While you are at it, head over to www.CrackBerry.com and become register on that site as well. Members can learn new things, download cool files and programs, and immediately become a part of the biggest BlackBerry user community on the Internet.

Ok, enough shameless plugs. We sincerely hope that you learned a great deal from reading this book, and that you can now formulate a plan to better manage your life and your BlackBerry without causing unnecessary pain to those you work with and those you love. We, the authors, learned a great deal when writing this book, as well! Each of us has recognized the signs of addiction, and each of us has resolved to follow the steps outlined in this book in a bid to live a BlackBerry-balanced life.

So remember, these rules are just a start. We can do more. For example, we can also make some life changes that will improve our quality of BlackBerry life—for both ourselves and all those around us.

To guide us along the path of BlackBerry overuse recovery, let's review our *BlackBerry Twelve Step* program before we part ways:

Step 1: Admit We Are Powerless Without Our BlackBerry

Step 2: Believe in Things More Important than Our BlackBerry

Step 3: Begin to Turn Away from our BlackBerry Abuse

Step 4: Take a Moral Inventory of Our BlackBerry Abuses

Step 5: Admit to Our Specific BlackBerry Abuses

Step 6: Plan to Be a More Responsible BlackBerry User

Step 7: Ask for Help in Achieving Responsible BlackBerry Use

Step 8: List Those BlackBerry Bystanders We Have Wronged

Step 9: Make Amends to Our BlackBerry Bystanders

Step 10: Adhere Tirelessly to the Rules of BlackBerry Etiquette

Step 11: Reflect to Reconnect With Others Around Us

Step 12: Resolve to be Responsible and Spread the Word

Living by these 12 Steps is certainly a start. Doing so will make our lives fuller and more varied, and it will help us achieve a greater sense of balance in our lives. There is more we can do, however.

CrackBerry Terms and Definitions

This appendix defines key words and phrases that every BlackBerry user and abuser should know.

Term	Definition
Battery Pull / Hard Reset	The first step in troubleshooting a network, software, or hardware error (as typically seen with a constantly spinning **Hourglass** icon or an ever-present **Timer** icon on the screen) is often to perform a *hard reset*. To do this, remove the battery while the device is still powered on, wait 30 seconds, and then reinsert the battery.
BB, 'Berry	These are commonly used nicknames for the BlackBerry smartphones.
BBOS	This is an abbreviation for the BlackBerry operating system, the on-device software that powers your BlackBerry. At publishing time, the newest generation BlackBerry smartphones use OS of version 6.0 or higher.

Term	Definition
Bedside Mode	This feature is present on BBOS version 4.6 and later (e.g., on the Bold, Pearl Flip, and Storm BlackBerrys). The addition of **Bedside** mode in the native **Alarm Clock** application lets the user disable the LED and/or radio and dim the screen to minimize potential distractions from the device while sleeping.
BlackBerry Messenger, BBM	The **BlackBerry Messenger** app (BBM) provides BlackBerry users with the familiar look-and-feel of a desktop instant messaging program right on the device. This program enables BlackBerry users to communicate directly with other BlackBerry users through PIN messaging, so long as both parties have a BlackBerry data plan. Unlike SMS, there are no per message charges; such messages are sent through RIM's internal servers.
BlackBerry Prayer	This is the position one often takes when emailing on a BlackBerry: head down, both hands in front of the body grasping the phone, and thumbs tapping at the keyboard while wearing a subtle look of concentration, combined with relaxed expression. To the onlooker, it appears as though the BlackBerry user is praying.
Bluetooth	Bluetooth is a wireless protocol utilizing short-range communications technology that facilitates data transmission over short distances from fixed and mobile devices. This technology creates wireless personal area networks (PANs). Within the world of BlackBerry, Bluetooth typically refers to peripherals used in conjunction with the BlackBerry, such as Bluetooth headsets that allow you to talk on your BlackBerry in a hands-free fashion.
CrackBerry	Slang term for a person who uses a BlackBerry smartphone addictively or obsessively or a term for the BlackBerry device itself when used this way
CrackBerry Prayer	See *BlackBerry Prayer*.
Desktop Manager	This is software from Research in Motion that is installed on one's desktop Windows computer. Desktop Manager software enables a user to carry out a number of BlackBerry management tasks, including the syncing of personal data, the creation of backups, the loading of applications, and more.
Facebook	This is a popular social networking website. Visit it at www.facebook.com.

Term	Definition
Flikr	This is a popular photo sharing website. Visit it at www.flikr.com.
GPS	GPS is an abbreviation for *global positioning system*. BlackBerry smartphones either contain a GPS chip, or they can connect to a Bluetooth GPS puck. With GPS enabled, the BlackBerry smartphone's location can be used by BlackBerry applications, such as navigation programs.
Holster	This is a case designed specifically for the BlackBerry that provides protection to the device, yet also enables easy, one-handed removal of the device. BlackBerry-specific holsters often contain a *sleeper magnet* that automatically places the BlackBerry into a battery conserving **Standby** mode.
Memory Leak	This refers to unintentional memory consumption on the BlackBerry, resulting in a lack of available resources. A lack of free memory results in poor or non-existent performance, and *buggy* behavior in general. A device suffering from a memory leak might show a spinning **Hourglass** icon or an ever-present **Timer** icon. Performing a hard or soft reset typically restores a device's memory.
MMS	This is an abbreviation for Multimedia Messaging Service. MMS allows you to create messages that are sent from one mobile device to another. Such messages may contain text, pictures, audio, and video.
PDA	This is an abbreviation for personal digital assistant. PDAs were the precursor to smartphones (think: Palm Pilot).
PIN	PIN is an acronym for personal identification number. A PIN is a unique, eight-digit alpha-numeric code that is assigned to every BlackBerry device. You can find your PIN code by going to Options > Status > PIN. If you know the PIN of another BlackBerry user, you can send messages to her device directly through RIM's servers. Instead of composing an email, you create a new PIN message. Your PIN number is often used to register software, so that it will only run on your specific BlackBerry.
Power Key	This is the end call **Red Phone** key (sometimes this key is at the top of the device) on the BlackBerry. This key also serves as the power on / off switch. Please note that turning the BlackBerry off using this button does not fully power down the device.

Term	Definition
Profiles	Profiles control the multiple notification alerts on a BlackBerry smartphone, such as incoming calls, emails, and SMS and **BlackBerry Messenger** messages. Default profiles include **Loud** (high volume, vibrate before ringing) and **Silent** (it mutes all notifications). A user can customize native profiles or create his own to customize the device to suit personal preferences.
Push / Pull Email	*Push* email refers to automatically transmitting email messages that have been received by a server mail system directly to a mobile device at the time the email arrives on the server. *Pull* email refers to the process whereby the mobile device periodically checks the mail server for new messages, whether or not any new messages have arrived at the server.
QWERTY Keyboard	On a smartphone, QWERTY or full QWERTY refers to a keyboard that contains one key for every letter of the alphabet; it is akin to the standard keyboard used with a computer.
Red Blinking Light	When a BlackBerry smartphone receives a new message, the default setting is for the LED notification to blink *red* until the message is checked.
RIM	RIM is the abbreviation for Research in Motion, Ltd., the manufacturer of BlackBerry smartphones. We hope they read this book with a sense of humor!
Silent Mode	See *Profiles*.
Smartphone	There is no standardized definition for a smartphone. However, this term commonly refers to the merger between a traditional PDA and a standard cell phone. Many of these devices are so packed with functions that they approach the functionality of a laptop computer in a device that fits snugly in your hand.
SMS Text, SMS, Texting	SMS is an abbreviation for Short Message Service, and it is commonly referred to as *text messaging*. This feature is available with practically all modern mobile phones, and it allows users to send and receive short text messages. *Texting* is the act of sending an SMS text message.

Term	Definition
Soft Reset	Performing a soft reset stops all applications on the BlackBerry device. You press the **ALT** + **Right CAP** + **Delete** keys simultaneously on the BlackBerry keyboard to execute a soft reset. (*Note that this feature only works on BlackBerry smartphones with a single letter on each key of the keyboard.*)
SureType Keyboard	Through an integrated keyboard and software system, SureType effectively combines a traditional phone keypad and a familiar QWERTY-based keyboard to create an efficient and familiar typing experience.
Texting while driving	The refers to the act of sending a test message while behind the steering wheel of a car in motion. *This is not recommended!*
Trackball	Often referred to as the Pearl (the name of the BlackBerry smartphone it debuted on), the trackball is the round, rolling ball on the front side of the device. It is located below the screen, which allows for easy navigation. The trackball replaced the side-mounted *trackwheel* found on older BlackBerry smartphones. The trackball allows for both left- and right-handed use of the device.
Trackpad	Featured on BlackBerry smartphones after the Trackball. The trackpad has no moving parts and is mounted on the front of the device between the menu key and Escape key. The Trackpad allows the user to move the cursor around the screen, click to select items and other commands that require movement. With the Trackpad on the front of the device, it allows both left- and right-handed use.
Trackwheel	Featured on BlackBerry smartphones prior to the debut of the trackball on the Pearl, the trackwheel is mounted on the right side of the device. This component allows the user to move the cursor vertically or horizontally when the Alt key is pressed. Pushing or clicking the trackwheel selects objects or opens the menu.
Vibrate, Buzz	As an alternative to audible ringtones, BlackBerry smartphones feature the ability to vibrate or shake the phone. This vibration signals the device's user that she has an incoming call or message.

Term	Definition
WI-FI	This term refers to certain types of wireless local area networks that use specifications in the 802.11 family. In regards to smartphones, Wi-Fi refers to the ability of a device to connect to the Internet through a local connection, rather than through the wireless carrier's network. No data charges are incurred when on Wi-Fi. If a BlackBerry has Wi-Fi, a Wi-Fi logo is displayed in the upper part of the **Home** screen.
YouTube	This is a popular video sharing website.

Index

You Need the Companion eBook

Your purchase of this book entitles you to buy the companion PDF-version eBook for only $10. Take the weightless companion with you anywhere.

We believe this Apress title will prove so indispensable that you'll want to carry it with you everywhere, which is why we are offering the companion eBook (in PDF format) for $10 to customers who purchase this book now. Convenient and fully searchable, the PDF version of any content-rich, page-heavy Apress book makes a valuable addition to your programming library. You can easily find and copy code—or perform examples by quickly toggling between instructions and the application. Even simultaneously tackling a donut, diet soda, and complex code becomes simplified with hands-free eBooks!

Once you purchase your book, getting the $10 companion eBook is simple:

❶ Visit **www.apress.com/promo/tendollars/**.

❷ Complete a basic registration form to receive a randomly generated question about this title.

❸ Answer the question correctly in 60 seconds, and you will receive a promotional code to redeem for the $10.00 eBook.

THE EXPERT'S VOICE™

233 Spring Street, New York, NY 10013

Offer valid through 3/11.